*Praise for Sara Wiseman's*
# Writing the Divine

"Sassy and approachable, *Writing the Divine* is a great read filled with practical information on how to listen for the messages from the divine. But take it seriously. There is wisdom in this work. *Highly recommended.*"

—Sophy Burnham,
author of *New York Times* bestselling *A Book of Angels*

"*Writing the Divine* is the best book out there on the subject of channeled writing. It's comprehensive, informative, inspiring, authentic, funny, and one of the most well written and detailed how-to books I've had the pleasure of reading. Sara's down-to-earth and open-hearted approach makes the subject matter even more compelling."

—Debra Lynne Katz, professional psychic and
author of *You Are Psychic* and *Freeing the Genie Within*

"Wiseman beautifully lays down the stepping stones to help us on our soul's homecoming to Divinity. She lovingly shares with us the treasures of divine guidance entrusted her by spirit, while gracefully offering us wisdom culled from her own experience of spirit and of practicing The 33 Lessons. Wiseman shines in teaching us the true purpose of life: our soul growth."

—Michael J Tamura, visionary teacher, spiritual healing pioneer,
clairvoyant, and award-winning author of *You Are the Answer*

"In *Writing the Divine*, Wiseman demystifies the channeling process, making a sacred act simple. With wit and delightful humor, she shares practical tools for connecting with the divine inner voice."

—Vicky Thompson, editor of *New Connexion Journal*
and author of *Life-Changing Affirmations*

# Writing
## the
# Divine

## About the Author

Sara Wiseman experienced a spiritual awakening in 2004, when she unexpectedly received channeled writing from a spirit guide. Four years later, she received The 33 Lessons, an intensive experience of channeled writing that begins, "The purpose of life is soul growth." Today, she teaches a *direction connection* to the Divine via workshops and private consultation. Prior to this, Wiseman was a commercial writer and journalist. A singer/songwriter, she has released three CDs with her band, Martyrs of Sound: *Mantra Chill, Uncoiled,* and *Songs for Loving & Dying.* She lives in Oregon with her family and may be reached at www.sarawiseman.com.

How to Use Channeling
for Soul Growth & Healing

# Writing
## the
# Divine

*Experience 33 Lessons for Divine Guidance*

# Sara
# Wiseman

Llewellyn Publications
Woodbury, Minnesota

First Edition
First Printing, 2009

Cover design by Lisa Novak
Cover image © 2009 iStockphoto.com/friztin
Editing by Nicole Edman

Llewellyn is a registered trademark of Llewellyn Worldwide, Ltd.

**Library of Congress Cataloging-in-Publication Data**
Wiseman, Sara, 1962–
  Writing the divine: how to use channeling for soul growth & healing /
by Sara Wiseman.—1st ed.
      p. cm.
  Includes bibliographical references.
  ISBN 978-0-7387-1581-0
  1. Channeling (Spiritualism)  I. Title.
  BF1286.W57 2009
  133.9'1—dc22
                                  2009019486

Llewellyn Publications
A Division of Llewellyn Worldwide, Ltd.
2143 Wooddale Drive, Dept. 978-0-7387-1581-0
Woodbury, MN 55125-2989, U.S.A.
www.llewellyn.com

Printed in the United States of America

This book is dedicated to my late father,
Dr. Harry R. "Bud" Knudson, Jr.
and my mother, Sallye Knudson.

# Contents

# Part Two: The 33 Lessons

# Acknowledgments

IF THERE'S ONE THING I learned during the experience of receiving and writing this book, it's that nothing happens without the support and love of others. We are here to help each other on our paths, and I am grateful to everyone who has stepped forward to help me take each next step—especially the friends who dragged me out of the brambles, pointed me in the right direction, and sent me on my way.

I wish to thank my amazing children, who gave me the space to write and encouraged me to keep going.

I am eternally indebted to my partner, Dr. Steve Koc, who believed in The 33 Lessons from the very beginning and stood right beside me as I wrestled with the task of receiving them and writing this book. And, for showing me how to make music. Thank you.

Finally, thanks to a few people who've been supportive beyond reason: Sophy Burnham, Jason Carter, Terri Daniel, Erin Donley, Nicole Edman, Krista Goering, Dan Goodman, Hollee Haas, Debra Lynne Katz, Eric Knudson, JoAnne Kohler, Gregory Kompes, Carrie Obry, Dr. Prasanna Pati, Steven Pomije, Penny Sansevieri, Michael Tamura, Vicky Thompson, Leslie Venti, Gary Weber, and Susan Wisehart. I am grateful to you all.

# Preface

I DID NOT INTEND TO write this book.

In the spring of 2008, I was happily enmeshed in the plot intricacies of my third novel, when I received several clear messages to put aside my novel—because another project was about to arrive.

This did not make me happy! I loved my novel, was deep into its writing, and was certain that I had no higher calling than to write it.

But certain persistent spirit guides had other plans. The result was that in March 2008, after receiving so many signs and synchronicities that they could no longer be dismissed, I returned to my practice of channeled writing, which I'd begun four years earlier but had sorely neglected.

Why had I stopped?

In a nutshell, because I thought I already knew what I was supposed to be doing—writing my novel! Nonetheless, I resumed my practice of channeled writing with trepidation one solitary Saturday morning when my family was out of the house. I plugged in my laptop, settled on the sofa, closed my eyes, and began taking the deep breaths that would take me into a channeled trance.

I've been in this trance state many times—it's as natural to me as breathing or sleeping. I like to think of this state as similar to deep relaxation. It's the same place you go when you pray or meditate, or right before you go to sleep at night, or upon your first dreamy awakening in the morning. There's nothing tricky about it, and nothing difficult about going there once you get the hang of it. As for the channeling part? For me it's very easy—like switching on a radio, tuning into a clear station, and settling back to hear your favorite program.

Except this time, the program was unfamiliar.

Moving uneasily within my trance state, I tried to reconnect with that familiar voice I'd heard in the past (his name is Hajam, and I'll tell you the whole story in chapter three). In vain, I listened for this particular spirit guide who'd come forth when I'd practiced channeled writing before; the comforting soul who was my personal champion and teacher.

Except he didn't show.

Instead, I saw and heard a new guide, an older woman in drab clothing whose name I would learn was Constance. My purpose for this channeled writing session, I understood, was to channel what Constance (and eventually, two other entities) had to say.

"Lesson One," Constance began, "The purpose of life is soul growth." I keyed her words cautiously on my laptop. "There will be *thirty-three lessons*." I ducked my head, took a deep breath, and kept going, too surprised to stop.

Constance?

*Thirty-three lessons?*

Where was my dear, familiar guide? Why wasn't I hearing from *him*? I felt like I'd bought a ticket to Jackie Chan's *Shanghai Noon*, and now they were showing Cecile B. DeMille's *Ten Commandments*! Obviously, my little posse-of-one had galloped far over the next hilltop and was nowhere to be seen. Constance was the leading lady here, and she was a serious, intense presence. It was clear that she expected me to sit up and take notice.

So I did.

I channeled in a trance as time suspended, caved in on itself, and finally dissolved. I do not know exactly how long I sat there and typed, listening carefully for Constance's exact words. Her voice came in clearly through my right ear—not as an outer voice, but as a voice within my own voice, a voice that was not my own. When Constance finally stopped speaking, I came out of my trance, looked at what I'd written, and saw I'd completed twenty pages in one sitting.

For those of you who are writers, getting one good page done is sometimes a miracle—and here Constance had given me twenty! My hands were cramped, my back was numb, and my head was spinning. I understood, without a doubt, that I was to return to channel the next lesson the following day.

I shut down my laptop without even bothering to read what I'd keyed, then wandered around in shock for the rest of the day, considering what had happened:

- I had a new guide,
- I was receiving Lessons,
- I had no idea why, how, or what for
- there would be thirty-three of them, and
- the Lessons were meant for the world.

Why me? Why thirty-three? Why for the world?

As I considered my assignment—for yes, it was an assignment—it also dawned on me that the biggest cosmic joke of all (and there are many) is that just when you think you've finally figured out what you're supposed to be doing (e.g., writing your novel), you discover that you are quite definitely supposed to be doing . . . something else.

Still, I was beyond surprised when, after two weeks of channeled writing during which I took down Lesson after Lesson from Constance, I got an unexpected email from a literary agent.

"I've got a crazy idea for you," the agent wrote. "Are you interested in writing a book on channeling?"

Now, I may not be the quickest on the uptake re: the workings of the cosmos, the most up-to-date on string theory, or the most erudite on how to piece together the universal puzzle, but this particular synchronicity was not lost on me.

"Yes," I emailed back. "As a matter of fact, I am."

And thus, this book was born. Part Constance's and the other entities', part mine; meant for the world, for soul growth and healing.

PART ONE

# Writing the Divine

# 1

⌒

# What Is Channeling?

*Channeling is a direct connection to the Divine that is a two-way com-munication between the person channeling and the Divine. Channeling may be received as a voice, sound, word, music, image, picture, diagram, vision, sign, synchronicity, or other.*

Gulp. Two-way communication? Not just you talking to *them*, but *them* talking to you? Yep, that's right.

This entire concept of a two-way communication with the Divine can be a little mind-blowing. Certain religions probably forbid it out-right. Lots of people will tell you that you can't do it by yourself—that you need a medium, psychic, priest, guru, or other "translator" to make the connection.

Don't listen to them.

When I first became aware of this avenue of connection, I felt it couldn't be real. How could something so simple, yet perhaps the most important tool that I'd ever used, be so unknown? Why didn't anyone talk about it? Why wasn't it shouted from the rooftops, plas-tered on every billboard, taught in the schools, franchised on every street corner like Starbucks?

Well, let's see . . .

When I first started channeled writing in 2004, I didn't talk about my experience with any of the people I knew then, because I was pretty sure they'd think I'd gone nuts. What do you say to the guy in the next cubicle at work, or the parents from the soccer team?

"Hi, nice tie, and by the way, God's talking to me. No, I mean, God's *really* talking to me. He arrives in the form of my own personal spirit guide, and he comes to my house every day and . . ."

Not the best conversation-starter for Monday morning at the water cooler, or for standing on the sidelines watching the Sharks devour the Minnows.

"What a game! We're really creaming 'em, aren't we? Did I mention I've been talking to God? No, not at church—at my house. Does he talk back? Why, yes he does. What does he say? Oh, mostly telling me how to fix my problems and . . . hey, you're leaving already? It's only the first quarter."

You get the idea.

Too much of this I-talk-to-God stuff, and after a while, your friends start doing that sheepish little wave from across your kid's classroom, and they don't invite you to participate in the Spring Plant Sale anymore.

So for a very long time, I kept mum. I mumbled and evaded about my channeled writing—I certainly didn't mention I was receiving messages called The Truths, or later, The 33 Lessons.

It wasn't until people began showing up in my life via the writing workshops that I taught (and frankly, everywhere else I went) that I began to see how desperately channeling was needed. People who had giant boulders smack dab in the middle of their life's path would arrive unexpectedly on my doorstep. These folks needed answers! And while I didn't know their answers, I sure as heck knew where they could find them.

Yet, even with the universe sending me a steady stream of folks who needed exactly what channeling and channeled writing had to offer, it took me a long time to understand that I was supposed to write about it, I was supposed to talk about it, and I was supposed to teach it.

Now, I'm grateful I can offer these tools to the world. Channeling isn't going to fit for everyone, and that's okay. But for some people, these tools are going to be exactly, perfectly right . . . and they'll discover them at the right time, just when they are ready to remove a very large boulder from their path.

## Do You Have to Be Psychic to Channel?

Well, that's a trick question. First of all, everyone is psychic, although some people have different aspects of this gift. So, yes, you have to be psychic—but without lifting a finger, you already are. You were born psychic, even if you haven't exercised your psychic muscles in a long time, or ever.

I'd like to say that one more time, so it will really sink in: *you don't need any special knowledge, abilities, or skills to channel.* Even if your psychic muscles are as flabby as a couch potato's, you'll do fine.

You also don't have to be trained in the mystic arts, have the ability to self-levitate, and so forth . . . you just have to ask for it to happen.

You can channel, your neighbor can channel, even people you don't like very much can channel, too (like I said, it's an equal opportunity technique). Channeling is no big deal, once you know how. What's more, the information you receive from channeling is not "in your imagination" or made up by your subconscious mind. It comes from the Divine direct to you, as if you'd found a giant, mystic radio station playing a program meant for your ears alone.

## Tuning In

When you first start to channel, you may have trouble hearing your messages clearly—I'll show you how to turn up the volume. Even after you've channeled for a while, you might have trouble understanding your messages—I'll explain how to gain more clarity.

You'll learn how to identify where Divine guidance is coming from—via a primary spirit guide, as was my experience when I first started. Or you may receive messages from a whole slew of spirit guides and angels. You may receive messages from Jesus, Buddha, the saints, any of the many Holy Ones that your particular religious affiliation or past religious tradition makes your heart long for.

While most of you will receive channeling as a voice or sound, some of you will receive images or other types of communication. As you delve deeper into this book, you'll learn about different ways of receiving. You'll learn the hands-on practice of channeled writing, whether you write on a laptop or use pen or pencil. We'll also talk about how to use a journal to support your channeling practice, and you'll learn how to manifest in writing—which is not a two-way communication with the Divine, by the way, but a specific request of the universe.

You'll learn how to do it all, simply and easily, no Ph.D. in metaphysics required.

## Respect the Connection

Channeling is serious spiritual business. When you open up a connection to the Divine, you open up a connection within the whole universal web of conscious connectedness. This isn't like going into a chat room and pretending you're somebody you're not. It's not like blogging either, where you send your messages out onto the World Wide Web and never know who reads them.

Channeling is more like calling God on the phone . . . collect . . . and yes, he's in, and yes, he'll pickup, and by the way, God has quite a bit to say to you!

"Hello, God here. Is that you?"

"OMG," you answer in shock, "is this really you, God?" You never thought you'd get God on the line!

"So I hear you want to know if you should quit your job?" God asks—and frankly, you're a little surprised she knows about that already. "I'll answer that question . . . but let's talk about your relationship problems first."

No messing around with God. She's got you pegged. When you call up looking for answers, be prepared for some straightforward direction.

Channeling is a gutsy act. It's you, one tiny milliparticle of ectoplasm in a vast infinite universe, daring to reach out your hand and turn on the Divine radio station. And the minute your hand touches that dial, the station's not only turning on, but it's tuning you in. This is a kind of energy that is beyond what most of us have experienced. It's bigger than you. It's the Now, in living color, in your very own living room.

Treat this connection with the utmost respect.

## Warnings and Advisements

- If you're interested in channeling darker spirits, mischievous tricksters, or have harmful intent to others, please stop reading this book. You're wasting your time here. The method of channeling in this book is designed only for the purpose of Highest Good for all. Its intent is only for those who are serious about seeking spiritual guidance and who have serious questions about their life's path, their purpose and passion, and the healing of their heart. This method of channeling is only for those who are willing to stand naked before the Divine.

- If you are reading this book and have a heavy heart, are consumed with grief or regret, or have lived a life that you are not proud of, have addictions, have issues, have problems, have made a mess of your life, have made mistakes you can fix, and are willing to try, even just one more time, please read on. And by the way, welcome to Club Human!

The Divine is perfect. We, earthbound, ragged, tormented, are not. Yes, our souls are in a perfect state, but we, as humans—it's a fact, we struggle. We also blunder, make mistakes, and after we've made all the mistakes that we possibly can, we compound the problem by making these exact same mistakes again.

- If you have mental heath issues or are currently in a delicate emotional state, please talk with a professional counselor before you try channeling. As we've discussed, channeling is a powerful tool and will bring change into your life. If you are especially fragile, it may be too much to take on at this moment in your life. Prayer and meditation will be ideal ways for you to receive Divine comfort at this time.

By now, a certain percentage of readers have thrown this book across the room, while the rest of you are champing at the bit. "All right already!" you say. "Show me how!"

So let's begin.

## 2

⟐

# Why Channel?

Have you ever wished you knew what your life's purpose was? Not just "sort of" knew, or had a vague idea, but really knew—the same way you'd know if someone came right up to you and whispered your life's purpose in your ear, or wrote it on a giant billboard for you to read, no second guessing required?

Have you ever tripped on your life's path, wishing someone would suddenly pull out a big road map labeled "Your Life," and pointed to a street you've never noticed before and direct loudly, "Go here!"?

Have you ever been in the midst of a deep heartbreak or sorrow or confusion, and wished there was someone you could turn to who had all the answers?

Or, perhaps you are one of the fortunate few who *has* discovered your life's purpose. In fact, you're clearly walking your life's path right now, head held high, energetically hiking along with your knapsack loaded with Luna bars and water, plus a box of bandages in case you get a blister, entirely confident of your life's direction. Until you reach a certain fork on your hiking trail and realize *you don't know which way to go.* Should you turn left? Should you head right? It's unclear which is the better path. You still want to reach your destination—but you can't figure out how to get there.

Or perhaps, as you stride purposefully along, a massive boulder appears in the middle of your path. There's no way over it, under it, around it. You're stuck, blocked by this giant rock. And as you sit there considering your options, you realize that not only are you stuck, but your surroundings are starting to look unfamiliar—the mountain, the path, the distant storm clouds—you're not sure you've seen them before. You swallow down your panic, as you realize that perhaps, maybe, quite possibly, you're a little bit lost. That boulder looks bigger than ever. Those storm clouds are definitely heading your way. You have a blister on your left heel, and it hurts. Furthermore, you have eaten all your Luna bars, and your water situation looks grim.

Right then and there, you probably wish you could call upon somebody who could give you a little help on this hiking path of life—that you could knock on the door of some rustic little mountain hut, and a wizened old gnome of a mountain man with a white beard hanging down to his belly button would come out and tell you exactly how to get to the place you were supposed to be going.

"You're going east?" this kindhearted person might say, shaking his head. "Oh no, comrade—you're supposed to be heading west."

"You're trying to go around the boulder?" this gnarled mystic might ask, stroking his long, fluffy beard. "Oh no, my friend. You need to forgive it."

In a single lucid flash, you'd understand these instructions exactly and precisely, and instantly you'd be back on track, on your life's path, with more energy than ever and not a storm cloud in sight.

And what about those of you who have been abused, molested, or harmed in this life, all of you who struggle with addictions, alcoholism, overeating, gambling, pornography? What about the many of you who've been stunned by divorce, separation, illness, or death? Do you ever wish there was a way to finally heal? To get past all the pain and grieving, and begin again as a new person, free from that damaging past?

I'm happy to tell you, there is.

The answer is one that will allow you to heal your body and your spirit, one that will allow you to live a life of comfort and abundance, have relationships that are harmonious and supportive, and enjoy work that you find meaningful. A life filled with love, purpose, and soul growth.

In fact, the answers to what you need to know so desperately are not particularly hard to receive. *You just need to know how to hear them.*

Perhaps you've tried religion, or you've numbed yourself with various addictions. Perhaps you've limped your way through a string of relationships that haven't worked out. You've shopped your way into debt, and eaten your way into a body that makes you feel deeply unhappy. Or maybe you're doing okay by most people's standards—you've got a great house, a great car, money in the bank. You've Botoxed and tummy-tucked until you look younger than you did when you actually *were* younger.

But nothing, repeat nothing, seems to help.

That's because *there is no answer from the outside.* There is no person, no motivational speaker, no guru, no priest, no doctor, no psychologist, no life coach, no psychic, no call-in radio show, no religion, no book, no DVD set, no health club, no weight-loss program, no drug, no food, no adventure, no trip, no bank balance, no twelve-step meeting, no corporate success program, no way of changing your appearance or house or car that can help.

The answer to all you need lies with another source entirely.

The answer to everything you need to be happy, to live a life of purpose and passion, is not found through another teacher, book, or program.

Instead, it's found very simply—so simply it almost seems impossible—with a *direct connection* to God, the Divine, the universe, the cosmos, the Source—all the names we use when we talk about the infinite presence of Now.

You'll notice I am not asking you to leave your religion, convert to a new religion, or alter your belief system in any way.

If you believe in Jesus, please believe in Jesus. If you're into Kabbalah or Buddhism or Hinduism, please continue. If you're an agnostic or don't know what you are, or you used to go to church but you haven't been in a while—welcome aboard. Atheists? Plenty of room for you, too.

A *direct connection* will work for you—even if you don't believe it will.

## Why Not Use Prayer or Meditation?

Now, I can sense that some of you are muttering and shaking your heads, especially those of you who already have a regular practice of prayer or meditation. Please, before you throw this book against the wall, allow me to clarify: *prayer and/or meditation are incredible tools for changing your life.* If you pray or meditate regularly, please continue with these practices!

Prayer is one of the sweetest, most comforting ways of talking to God.

However, there are many people who have been wounded by the misguided efforts of religions—28 percent of Americans have left the faith they were raised in, and 44 percent have changed their religious affiliation in their lifetime, according to a study by the Pew Forum on Religion and Public Life.[1] For you, the idea of prayer may have become so polluted by guilt, unhealthy tradition, or past damage that it may not be a tool that's acceptable to you right now.

Those who practice meditation understand its power—it calms you down, gets you focused, has numerous health benefits, and its regular practice is a pathway to spiritual enlightenment. *Just like prayer, there is no question that meditation works!* But so many people I've talked to

---

1 Pew Forum on Religion and Public Life, U.S. Religious Landscape Survey, February 2008.

say they "can't" focus—their mind races, their mantras don't work, they can't sit still, their back, hips, and legs hurt, and so on. In fact, one of the most beautiful, evolved women I know, a marvelously gifted floral designer who's traveled the world sharing her artistry and has authored numerous books on the subject, recently told me she can't meditate "because her mind won't stop." So be it.

Meditation's not her thing.

It might not be yours.

This is okay, too.

## Making a Direct Connection

There is another way that you can enjoy a *direct connection* to God, one that's different than prayer or meditation. It's called *channeling*, and it's very easy to do—so easy that once you know how, you can do it at work, if you have a few moments of private time. You can do it when you're out for a walk. You can even do it sitting in your car (as long as you're not driving!).

Channeling is a tool for receiving precise, Divine guidance on the questions and problems that are eating you up inside:

*Do I turn left or right on my life's path?*

*Divorce her or book a second honeymoon?*

*Travel to India or settle for Indiana?*

*Stay with the company or start my own business?*

You know what your questions are.

Channeling provides the immediate feedback and clear direction that you need. And it's a source you can return to again and again, infinitely, as many times as you want, throughout your life.

# Crystal Ball Not Required

Let's face it. Channeling's gotten a bad rap. It calls to mind turbaned mediums with false eyelashes and way too much rouge, gazing cryptically over crystal balls. And wouldn't you know it, just when you yourself lean forward, eager to see what lies within the misty globe, poof! Apparently, only Madame Zorba is cleared for crystal ball access.

Or perhaps you think of channeling as calling forth spirits from the dead in a séance or making objects fly around the room. These parlor tricks were popular in the late 1800s and early 1900s, when Spiritualism, a type of occult practice, was all the rage. But real channeling—authentic receiving for spiritual guidance—has nothing to do with crystal ball gazing. And it most certainly doesn't involve any kind of messages or images that only a "special" medium can hear or see.

That's the beauty of direct connection.

Because while the cosmos is a deep, unfathomable mystery, connecting with it is not. It's a process that can be as simple and automatic as breathing, eating, sleeping, and laughing.

Anyone can do it.

In channeling, there is no medium. There is no middleman. There is no guru, no priest, no tour guide.

It certainly doesn't cost any money.

No special skills or aptitudes are required.

*All that is required is a willingness to connect with the Divine and to receive guidance.* In channeling, you are simply asking the Divine to connect with you in a direct, understandable way—and you are doing your part of the bargain, by opening your heart and allowing yourself to receive as a channel. This opening, this asking, this requesting, allows the messages of your spirit guides, angels, and other spiritual beings and energies to move through you.

Again, why not just pray or meditate?

*Because channeling is different.*

# How Channeling Works

When you pray, you probably ask God for help in solving a problem, or express your gratitude for this beautiful life. This is wonderful, marvelous. Please, keep praying!

When you meditate, you most likely lock into the hum of the universe and experience bliss. Again, this is superb! Please, keep meditating!

When you channel, however, you are deliberately asking for a direct connection with the Divine. Furthermore, you are asking for specific guidance in the form of answers to your questions. When you channel Divine guidance, you will clearly understand what you should do next, what your life's purpose is, and what is the next step to take in following your life's path.

*Should I buy a new car or save the money in a mutual fund?*

Ask the Divine, and you'll hear the answer and know what to do.

*Should I leave my husband or go to a marriage counselor?*

You'll hear or see the answer through channeling, or be given signs, clues, and *strands* (more on this later) that point you in the right direction.

*Should I quit my job and start my own business?*

Channeling will make it clear.

*What is my life's purpose? How can I heal my heart? Will I ever be free of the pain of my divorce? Who are the people I need to forgive? How can I become whole?*

You'll receive the answers you need to know through channeling.

And what if God tells you something you don't want to hear?

Again, you'll receive the answers you need to know.

# 3

⟿

# An Unexpected Receiving

By the time I received The 33 Lessons from Constance, I'd been practicing channeled writing for some time. But the first time it happened, it almost knocked my socks off.

It all started in the summer of 2004—on the very morning that I moved into my new home as the first step of divorce. You've heard of hitting bottom? I'd long past hit bottom and was hurtling into the abyss.

After eighteen years of marriage and four kids, this was an unbelievably painful process that involved loading everything deemed "mine" from the family home into a rickety rental truck. Two burly movers, mouths dark with tobacco and reeking of beer and sweat, were there to do the heavy lifting.

I spent that morning in a state of numbness and disbelief, watching the movers haul things out my old house and dolly boxes into the gaping yaw of my new house. One mover even had the audacity to ask me out when he was done working.

"I'm moving here!" I felt like shouting. "I'm getting divorced here!" I wanted to scream, but I was too tired, too fragile, too heartbroken. I simply shook my head.

No.

After the movers left, I stood with my meager furniture in disarray, stacks of unmarked and unidentified boxes, black plastic trash bags stuffed full of toys and clothes after I'd run out of boxes, beds not only unmade but lacking mattresses (the kids and I would sleep on the floor that night), and everything piled in the wrong room.

Complete chaos.

Absolute pain.

Regardless of how I felt, I knew it was crucial to create some semblance of order before the kids came home from school—but I didn't know how to begin. The knife or scissors I needed to open all these boxes was packed in one of the boxes—but which one?

As I stood shakily in the living room, trying to get a grip on my roiling emotions, I looked out the front window and saw a man walking along the sidewalk. To my surprise, he headed up my driveway, and began climbing the steps to my front door.

He's in sales, I thought ungraciously—I certainly wasn't going to let him in.

Yet, this man didn't ring the doorbell or knock. Instead, he stood there patiently, hovering outside the front door. And finally, as I stood in the living room not breathing, hoping and praying he'd go away, he opened the door and stepped inside.

Let me explain.

He did not "open" the door in the same physical way that you or I or another human being might. I did not "see" him as a physical person exactly, even though I could easily describe what he looked like. Back then, I didn't even know enough to recognize him as a spiritual entity. But there he was, as clearly as anyone might be—my sense of him was overwhelming.

I was pretty sure he wasn't a ghost. He wasn't a trickster, either. Although I knew very little about this kind of thing, having spent the last decade of my life at kids' soccer games, not séances, I knew enough to understand this "being" was the real thing—I just didn't know what kind of real thing he was.

This "being" walked or floated or moved across the floor of my living room, and it was then that I met my spirit guide, Hajam, for the first time.

He was a dark, slender Indian or Asian man, much smaller than me. He looked like a guru might, but without all the drapery and turbans. He looked like a guru, I might add—except at that time, I didn't know about gurus. I knew about angels, of course, and Jesus, and God the Father and the Holy Spirit—my Judeo-Christian upbringing had made sure of that—but this "being" had no wings. No halo. Nary a beard nor pair of sandals in sight!

I dropped onto the sofa, partly for fear my legs might buckle underneath me, and he sat near my shoulder. To further clarify, Hajam didn't exactly "sit" either, but sort of hovered patiently near me, until it dawned on me that he was going to say something.

Until this time I'd been a) stunned, b) fascinated, and c) terrified, but when I realized he was going to speak to me, I freaked out.

*Write it down!* I heard my writer's mind yell in panic. *Write down what he's going to tell you!*

I leapt up and raced around the house trying to find my laptop (a laptop is the one thing a writer will never lose in a packing box, and sure enough, there it was on the kitchen counter), all the time wondering if this man, or being, or whatever he was, would disappear.

"I've been under a lot of stress," I thought wildly. "This is all my imagination. When I come back in the room, he'll be gone."

But he was not.

Hajam was definitely, entirely there, and so I plugged in, sat down, closed my eyes (mostly because I too terrified to look at him), and waited. After a few moments, Hajam, the spirit guide hovering at my shoulder, there but not there, began to speak in a soft, melodic, strongly accented voice. And in this way, I received my first channeled writing.

# An Emerging Spirituality

Was this new to me? Absolutely yes . . . and no. Looking back, I see that I've always been mystically inclined—I just didn't have the vocabulary to know that's what it was. As a young child, I'd been obsessed with all things religious, prone to setting up little Buddhist altars in my room and praying endlessly to saints and angels.

I went to Catholic school, but I wasn't faithful to the creed—I checked out every book the local library had on religion and religious traditions: Jewish, Hindu, Muslim, Quaker, you name it, it was all fair game—and this was when I was in elementary school! I read all those books, literally stacks and stacks of them, because I wanted to find the perfect religion—but of course, I could never decide.

As I child, I believed that I had many mystic experiences—yet, I also had a rather vivid imagination—so it was very easy for my parents and teachers to dismiss things as imagined or made up.

My parents weren't religious. Agnostic, Presbyterian . . . I wasn't quite sure where they stood on the Belief-O-Meter. Spiritually, I'd been raised with a sort of benign neglect combined with flurries of intensive religious exposure: I never went to church with my parents, but as a young girl I attended an array of country churches each Sunday with my grandfather. Sometimes we'd drink grape juice out of little cups, sometimes we'd have wine from a communal goblet, sometimes there was no Communion. To further confuse me, my parents sent me to Catholic school in an ancient, saint-laden convent in Seattle—marble hallways, statues of Mary, sacred hearts of Jesus, nuns in wimples. I walked around in a state of ecstatic bliss through middle school, and I converted to Catholicism after my children were born—searching for that perfect religion again.

I enjoyed being a Catholic at the beginning—the prayer, the comfort, the community. But it was only a few years later that I began to hear from Hajam, and then I had to choose—what the church told me I should believe, or what I was experiencing of the Divine on my own, as a direct connection.

# Receiving The Truths

Of course, I'd had the help of spirit guides and angels before—all of us do, at all times. It's just that I'd never known this personally, experientially—I'd never seen or heard them for myself. Until I began channeled writing, I'd never made a direct connection with the Divine before in such a clear, unexpected way. And after I stopped being afraid, these visits from Hajam became some of the most beautiful, intense, blissful connections I have ever known.

Over a period of the next two months, not daily but often, Hajam arrived to me. I created the habit of sitting on the same sofa, an old, antique-store find I'd gotten for $125 when I'd moved. The pillows were ripped, and there was lovely nailhead trim around the legs, and it had a marvelous vibe, as if the people who'd owned it before had been people I'd have wanted to know. I'd sit there whenever I was lonely, anxious, or completely unsure of what my next step on life's path was to be, and meditate a little and pray a lot. I'd sit there and turn on my laptop, close my eyes, and wait for Hajam to appear.

When he came, and in those first few months of living on my own, he came every time I called, Hajam dictated to me The Truths, a series of writings on love, the Beloved, nature, trees, the small ironies and beauties of the world. On sex and energy and timelessness. Always his language was rich and poetic, filled with gorgeous imagery and heartbreaking meaning. Hajam gave me short, sweet writings—some a few paragraphs, some a few pages. Nothing too difficult. Nothing ugly. Only beauty, grace, love—exactly what my broken heart needed to know.

Interestingly, these Truths weren't anything like what I would receive later in The 33 Lessons (I'll share some of them in chapter eleven). They were entirely different messages—and exactly what I needed to hear.

I accepted them gratefully, balm to my wounded heart. Yet, at the same time, I also wondered if I might be going mad. As anyone who has gone through divorce knows, it's one of the most stressful events you can experience. I shared custody of my children and missed them beyond my heart's capacity when they were gone. I grieved the end of my marriage, which after many years of patching and applying layer after layer of spackle and duct tape, couldn't be repaired any more. And I was always afraid at night, waking up terrified at the smallest creak or bump, alone in the house after a lifetime spent living with other people.

Yet, as I waited upon Hajam's visits, I understood my life had changed. Suddenly, out of the blue, I was a channel. "I am a voice, I am a conduit." I wrote one day in my journal, and I understood that this was true.

It was confusing, after all these years of being mom, wife, worker, volunteer, Catholic, to suddenly realize I was a "channel." Why had this happened? Why had it happened to me?

Furthermore, when I received The Truths from Hajam, sitting on that old sofa (the same sofa I sit on even as I write this today,) I didn't know what to do with them. There were not enough to make a book. They spoke almost entirely of true love, and of finding one's Beloved. I certainly wasn't in the dating pool! How did this apply to me?

I had so many questions, I was so confused—so at some point during the channeled writing sessions, I began to ask questions.

"What's going to happen to me?" I asked Hajam. "What should I do next?" "How can I help my kids?" "What do I need to know?"

To my amazement, my questions were immediately answered.

I discovered that not only was Hajam a source for me to channel what *he* wanted me to receive (The Truths), but that he was also a source of complete comfort and guidance to me. To me personally! Hajam told me that he was my very own spirit guide, a Divine being who'd be with me until my time on this earth was over. And that I would always be able to reach him through channeling and channeled writing.

Now, years later and many miles on the spiritual path logged, I can reach Hajam, or any of the other angels who surround me, simply by calling them to me. They are available at all times; there is never a moment when they are not around.

I now understand that there is no difference between Hajam and other spirit guides who regularly support me, the angels, the archangels, God, Jesus, Buddha, the other saints and Holy Beings, the cosmos, the universe, the Now, the Source, the Divine, whatever name you choose to call it. It's all the same.

It's all God. All Now. All infinite, perfect, and sublime. It's all One. And we're part of it.

But I didn't know that back then.

Back then, in the summer of 2004, cosmic oneness was not in my field of awareness. I was shattered, sketchy, fragile, pretty much broken. I was in the process of shedding the cocoon of my former life, the only life I'd ever known, and this cocoon was wrapped very tightly around me. A butterfly trying to emerge? I felt more like a shackled moth.

Thus, channeled writing became my tool for accessing Divine guidance.

"How will I do this?" I'd write. "Is this the correct path?" "Are my children okay?" "Will I have enough money?" And later, "What will happen next?" "Will I eventually meet a man?"

Astonishingly, what Hajam and my angels told me would happen was what *did* happen, over and over and over again, so that when the time came, I even knew the place(s) I would eventually meet the man who would become my partner, months before we'd even met.

I saw and wrote about the house I would live in a year before I knew I was moving. I even wrote I was going to have a new dog! I not only knew these things were going to happen, but I saw them take shape right before my eyes, one thing falling into place right after another.

My guides, my angels, the Divine, the universe, arranged everything. All because I wrote to them. And they answered back.

The best news is, I'm not the only one who can do this. You can, too.

# 4

## Going Into the Field

Sometimes, it's all you can do to stand shivering on the side of the pool, dipping your big toe in and worrying about how cold the water's going to be.

Other times, it's better to rip off your towel and, with a big "whoo hoo," race to the water's edge and cannonball right in.

This is one of those times.

Yes, there's a lot you'll want (and need) to know about channeling—but right now, the best way to proceed is try it for yourself. You'll get a little taste of what the channeling experience is like, and we'll talk over the details later.

We'll start with something easy: a short channeling session, as a kind of warm-up. We won't get too complicated, and we won't stay *in the field*, as some folks call it, for very long.

If you've ever taken a class in meditation, you know that you don't start with forty days of sitting on the mountaintop; instead you work up to longer and longer stretches of meditation. You take it in stages, because at first your brain isn't used to that kind of focus.

So too, a little bit of channeling goes a long way in the beginning. That's why this first time, we're going to go in and get out, quickly, easily, comfortably, and without fear, and just see what happens. You'll get a taste of what's there, but you won't eat the full-course meal.

To start this channeling warm-up session, you'll need a little bit of time—at least thirty minutes uninterrupted. You'll also need a quiet space—a room you can go into and lock the door, or an empty house with nobody home. Don't forget to turn off your cell phone. These next few moments are for you alone, without distraction or interruption.

You've probably already cleared your space, but if you haven't, here's how: you're clearheaded, no TV in the background, no radio. It's quiet. You can play some soft ambient music if you'd like, the kind of thing you'd hear in yoga class, or when you're getting a massage. (If you need help finding music that's suitable, check my website, www. sarawiseman.com, for Mp3 downloads.) Or, simply enjoy the quiet. The air is clean. You can breathe easily in the room.

As a note of warning, and I say this from personal experience, if you try to channel under the influence (alcohol, drugs, triple-grande mocha with extra whip), it's going to backfire—and it could backfire big. You're going to pull up energies that you really do not want to deal with. Do you really need a meltdown, freak out, flood of bad memories, or sob session at this moment?

No, you do not.

Thus, please come to this session with respect and a clear head.

As we begin, remind yourself that this first time is going to be light and easy. Don't expect too much, although anything can happen. Think of it like this: You're walking up to some friends' house, and you're going to ring the doorbell. Your friends might be home, or they might be out running errands. It's no problem if they're not in—you'll come back later. You'll catch up with them soon.

It's no big deal what happens.

Of course, your friends might be home after all. They might open the door with big welcoming smiles, usher you in, give you a big hug, and say, "How are you? What's going on? What can I help you with today?"

If this should happen to you during this initial channeling session—if you should meet a spirit guide, angel, or other Divine being, please don't stop the channel! Just keep going; simply stay with it and see what happens.

## Read the Instructions First

These instructions are very simple, but go ahead and read them a few times so you understand how it's going to work. If you get confused or off-track during this channeling warm-up, just keep going. You don't have to do everything perfectly. In fact, just sitting in your room deciding you're going to try is the first step to successful channeling.

Here's what to do:

**Get comfortable.** If it works for you, sit on the floor with your legs crossed in front of you, as if you were about to meditate—some folks like this "lotus" position. Others find they can't move their body this way, or it hurts their back or legs. In that case, sit in a chair, on a sofa, or sit up in bed. The most important thing is to not get too slouched—you want to keep your spine straight, to allow your breath to support you.

Now, every yoga book in the world will tell you to "keep your back straight," and that's ideal. But again, we're human. If you can sit with your back straight, do so. If your muscles don't work that way or you find it's distracting or painful, sit as you can. Later on, in some portions of a deeply channeled trance, your body may actually go limp—if that happens, there won't be anything you can do. Don't worry about it.

At this point, what's most important is that you're in a comfortable and safe place, you have the time you need, and you have privacy. You have at least thirty minutes for this process, and you won't be disturbed. It's peaceful where you are, and you feel fine. You may be a little excited or nervous about what might happen next, and that's fine, too.

**Go into trance.** Close your eyes, take a deep breath in through your nose, let your belly fill up with air, and breathe out through your nose. Repeat this until you start to feel calmed down—just getting properly oxygenated is going to help. Don't worry about how long it takes you to complete a breath cycle. Simply breathe deeply, and when you're ready to exhale, breathe out. That's all. It's very easy, it's just breathing—you do it all day long! No stress or strain, nothing forced.

Take about twenty of these deep, relaxing breaths with your eyes closed. By this time, you will begin to enter a state of relaxation. Let your body relax completely—and again, while it's best to keep your back straight, your body might do something different. Continue breathing as you head into a deeper relaxed state. By this time, you'll be less aware of any distracting sounds around you. You'll just sink deeper and deeper into relaxation, and some of you may begin to enter a state of trance.

What is trance? Basically, it is an altered state of consciousness that arrives during deep levels of relaxation, prayer, and meditation; while dancing, singing, playing music, and listening to certain kinds of repetitive or tonal music; and in other experiences where your conscious mind lets go for a while.

Trance happens at the point in which you shift your consciousness from normal perception into awareness of the infinite, ever-expanding energy of the universe. Now, that's a lot of verbiage for what's a very accessible experience for most people—that's why I'll often call trance "going in" or "going under," as this helps people understand it better.

During this initial stage of channeling, people often tell me they have trouble relaxing their minds—their brains are so used to being busy thinking about this schedule, that activity, this errand, that deadline, and so on. If you find your mind is racing, looping, or obsessing, just keep breathing and mentally say to yourself: "Thanks, brain, for those reminders that I'm busy and have a lot to think about.

But I'm gonna take a little break from those thoughts now, okay? I'll come back to them, but right now, I'm going to take a breather." And watch as your mind gives you a little break.

You might find yourself resisting as your body begins to enter a relaxed state. If you've been using constant busyness as a way of preventing yourself from seeing the pain that's bubbling up under the surface—that pain that's going to rise up the minute you let your guard down—tell yourself: "This is just a warm-up. There won't be any pain. There might be pain later on, but not now." And watch as your body gives you a little break.

If you close your eyes and suddenly panic, thinking, "Oh no, this is prayer again," and it brings up concepts of sin or guilt or bad associations with a former religion, or if you think, "Oh no, this is meditating, and it's never worked for me," then tell yourself this: "I'm not praying here. I'm not meditating. I'm just going to channel, just a quick little warm-up, kind-of channel, and we'll see what happens." Tell yourself this, and watch as your mind settles itself.

**Adjust your level of trance.** If you spend a lot of time praying, so that the minute you close your eyes you start to feel the act of prayer coming on, then go ahead and pray for a while. And as you pray, ask God to help you as you head into this new experience of channeling.

Similarly, if you've done a lot of meditating and go into a deep trance right away, hold yourself back. Right before you begin to enter that deep tunnel of meditative state, shake yourself mentally and say, "I'm not going totally under today. I'm going to use my trance to do something different. Instead, I'm going to channel Divine guidance."

**Let go of fear.** For those people who are afraid that it's going to hurt, that if they allow their heart to open just one tiny little crack that their whole world will come tumbling down, just relax. That kind of pain is not going to happen this time—remember? It's just a practice session, it doesn't really count. You're just ringing the doorbell at your friends' house, checking to see if anybody's home.

**Ask to receive.** Now, take those twenty deep breaths, and as you feel yourself go into the relaxed state, say to yourself, "I'm ready to become a channel for Divine guidance today. I'm ready to receive any messages for the Highest Good. Please, tell me what I need to know."

Say these words aloud if you like, or in your head. Then, continue breathing deeply, in through the nose, filling the belly, out through the nose again, and wait to see what happens.

Spend some time just quietly breathing, listening, being aware that you have opened a channel and the Divine is paying attention. You're paying attention too, waiting to see what you might hear, see, know, or experience. If you see something, hear something, or notice anything, simply take notice of it. If you hear messages or see images, allow them to come. Simply let what happens happen.

**Close the channel.** After allowing yourself at least ten minutes in this state, whether or not you have heard anything or seen anything, or are not sure if you have or haven't, say "thank you" to the Divine, and then say aloud or to yourself, "I am closing the channel." If you've entered a trance state or feel very relaxed, stay inside that trance for as long as you like. When you are ready, come back to the world and open your eyes.

## What May Have Happened

Now, I can tell you that at this time, your spirit guides, your angels, whatever Divine beings you most identify with—they're excited. They're running around in their robes or caftans or saint outfits or whatever they wear, just wild with joy that you've called.

If you can't see or hear them yet, don't worry—we're only warming up. However, some of you *have* met your spirit guides already, and that's marvelous! Some of you will meet them soon. This is very exciting! Imagine you're a newborn, just pushed from the womb; you've just been laid on your mother's stomach, and now you're gazing for the first time into her adoring eyes. Now another face comes into focus, and you meet the eyes of your father, and he's crying with love for you.

That's the place you're in.

Your guides love you! They've watched you and helped you and supported you through all of this life; some of you have even been supported in previous lives by these same guides.

"If my guides are supporting me, why am I in such a mess?" you might ask, and it's a good question.

Maybe you haven't been paying attention to what they've been telling you, all these years. Or all these lives.

Or maybe you've never asked for their advice.

For example, what if you had access to perfect Divine knowledge all your life, and never asked a question? There you are in the classroom with God, Buddha, Jesus, whoever you choose to call the One, and yep, that's you in the back row, cracking jokes, popping gum, passing notes to your best friend, failing test after test, and never once raising your hand. For example:

"Um, God, can you tell me what to do here?"

"Yes, Bobby, I can," or "Yes, Barbara, I can."

It's just that simple—all the information is yours.

But instead, you don't ask. You don't listen. And you certainly don't stay after class to get help on a particularly difficult test question. You just sail out the door with your friends, certain that no teacher can help you.

All the while your teacher, your spirit guide, your angel, is standing there patiently.

"George, I have the answer you seek," or "Gina, please ask me."

But you don't. You're out the door. Gone.

*You must ask to receive answers.*

These aren't my rules. It's just how it works.

## What Else May Have Happened

Some of you will have met spirit guides or been filled with the presence of angels. You may have heard a voice in one ear or the other. You may have had the sensation of warmth, or a glow, or a sense of presence of something that is Not You. All of this is good.

However, if you're not sure what happened, or don't think anything happened, don't worry too much about it. It's just a practice. A warm-up.

For today, congratulate yourself! You picked up the phone and made the call to the Divine. You opened the channel and said you were willing to receive. Although this may seem elementary, this is plenty for one day.

As we move forward, you'll learn more about what to expect when you channel, what happens if you get confused, or what happens if you experience a direct connection.

Because the next time you practice, you're going all the way in.

# 5

A Brief History of Channeling
and Channeled Writing

Okay, you've got one channeling practice session under your belt. You're going to go into the field even further soon. You've experienced some things for yourself, and now you need more information.

Besides, you probably have some questions. *What happens next? What should I expect? What's a spirit guide anyway? Why didn't I see a spirit guide? When you say "angels," do you really mean angels? Who started this channeling stuff? What's channeled writing?* Understanding all these things requires more information and education, which is exactly what we're going to discuss next.

## Early Channeling Practices

Even though it seems strange and exciting, what we're doing is nothing new. Channeling's been around for centuries, a spiritual tool used by saints, priests, preachers, shamans, monks, and gurus in all times and cultures. The ancient mystics channeled: Rumi, for example, was in direct connection with the Divine as he wrote his poetry back in thirteenth-century Persia. Jesus and Buddha were master channelers—Divine beings themselves, they connected continually with the One.

In America, channeling enjoyed enormous popularity at the turn of the twentieth century, from the late 1800s to the early 1900s. There was an entire movement called Spiritualism, where people began to make connections with the spiritual realm on their own—by holding séances, by contacting the spirits of those who passed on, using Ouija boards, and so on.

Some of the work done during the Spiritualism movement was fake—parlor tricks, magic acts, sleight of hand. But quite a bit of it was serious, and although crystal ball gazing seems archaic now, many of those mediums paved the way for what was to come.

Some of the most groundbreaking pioneers during this time worked exclusively with channeled writing, at that time called "automatic writing" or "automat."

One particularly fascinating account is that of an ordinary woman, Margaret Cameron, who was playing with a Ouija board one evening, a popular entertainment during the Victorian era. (If you've never used a Ouija board, here's how it works: You place your hands lightly on a small tool called a planchette, which looks like a pointer on wheels. Then you allow your hand to be "guided" to the letters printed on the board to spell an answer.) To Cameron's astonishment, she was directed to specific letters, and soon discovered that these letters spelled words. She got so proficient at the Ouija board, she decided to try "automat" as she called it—receiving messages without the board.

It's interesting to note that back then, channelers were mostly concerned with contacting departed spirits—folks who'd recently died or lingering spirits who still had messages to pass on. The concept of contacting the Divine *directly* hadn't yet pervaded the collective consciousness.

# From Ouija Board to Automatic Writing

In the case of Margaret Cameron, she proceeded from Ouija board into automatic writing very quickly. Because there were no laptops or computers at this time, Cameron developed her own technique of using long rolls of wallpaper to record her automatic writing. Why? Because autowriting with your eyes closed can get messy! Your hand wanders and weaves around on the page, and many people find that they write each letter on top of the next. It's hard to read your Divine message if all you end up with is one big ink blob after thirty minutes of receiving. By working on long scrolls of wallpaper, Cameron was able to write left to right in a fairly legible way. As soon as each "automat" session was done, she'd type up the messages on a typewriter.

One of her most frequent channeled subjects was the spirit of a young man, Frederick, who'd recently died and wanted to reassure his family that he was fine. While it might seem a simple trick for a phony medium to fake messages from a dead relative, what happened in this situation was amazing. Cameron was able to receive this man's exact conversational style and lingo and details about people and events she'd never met or heard about, plus other information she couldn't possibly have known.

Through this spirit, she also received detailed information about what life was like after death, and how the entire channeling process worked—how spirits were able to make contact with humans and why it was sometimes difficult to understand them clearly.

She also was able to write, through Frederick, a series of lessons that discussed how we live on this earth, the forces of light and dark, the Great Purpose and more. Here, an excerpt of the writings she channeled:

> There are seven purposes. Progress, Light, Truth, Healing, Building, Production, and Justice. Equally great, save Progress, which moves them all. One of these must each man serve, if he proceeds toward the Great Purpose. Whether great or small, high

or low, wise or foolish, learned or ignorant, rich or poor, powerful or apparently impotent, each human individual is a force for construction or for disintegration, and follows his purpose to its inevitable end: constructive forces to construction of great purposes, disintegrating forces to the long struggle can have but one end, however distant—construction.

## Early Channeled Writings from Spirit Guides

Another autowriter from this era was M.A. (Oxon). These channeled writings were some of the few I found that did not contain messages from departed beings, but were received as a result of a direct connection with spirit guides.

Oxon's writing has a formal, almost religious tone that is similar to what might have been taught in the churches at the time, and yet the information is new—it hadn't been disseminated before. It might remind you of a sermon, but it doesn't contain information from the Bible. Instead, it matches more closely the content (but not the style) of A *Course in Miracles*.

Here, an excerpt from this fascinating work:

> Man—an immortal spirit, so we believe—placed in earth-life as a school of training, has simple duties to perform, and in performing them is prepared for more advanced and progressive work. He is governed by immutable laws, which if he transgresses them, work for him misery and loss; which, also, if respected, secure for him advancement and satisfaction.
>
> He is the recipient of guidance from spirits who have trod the path before him, and who are commissioned to guide him if he will avail himself of their guidance. He has within him a standard of right which will direct him to the truth, if he will allow himself to be guided to keep it and protect it from injury. If he refuses these helps, he falls into transgression and deterioration. He is thrown back and finds misery in place of joy. His sins punish themselves. Of his duties he knows by the instinct of his spirit as well as by the teaching of his guardians. The perfor-

mance of those duties brings progress and happiness. The spirit grows and gains newer and fuller views of that which makes for perfect, satisfying joy and peace.

Again, the tone's different, but the content is similar.

In the 1970s, *A Course in Miracles* was received by psychologist Helen Schucman, with help from psychologist William Thetford. This massive work took more than seven years to receive and record. It's been translated in many languages and is used by people all over the world as a spiritual teaching.

As you'd expect, these channeled writings are both celebrated and controversial.

I don't know how holy books from the ancient past were received—the Bible, the Torah, the Koran, the other holy texts of this world. Even scholars can't be sure. And yet surely these were channeled writings—the word of God, direct from God, as received by the channeler and recorded by his or her hand.

It is unclear to me why we would believe the authenticity of works that were channeled as "revelations" thousands of years ago, and yet refuse to think it is possible to receive authentic channeled works today.

Has the Divine stopped communicating with us?

Of course not.

Surely God comes to us in all ways, at all times, in all centuries, using the methods that we'll be most likely to hear and understand. Surely there is more ongoing holy wisdom than the ancient writings of the Bible, the Torah, the Koran, the teachings of the Tao.

## The Divine Uses Our Language

As the centuries roll forward, our language has become less flowery, less formal, and more slangy—and so too has the way in which God communicates with us. In the renowned *Conversations with God*, Neale Donald Walsch presents us with a very plainspoken voice of

God, nothing "thee and thou" about it. Jobless and suffering for many years, he was at home one day when God's voice just arrived to him.

Out of the blue. Without warning.

Fortunately Walsch was there on the other end, ready to listen and receive and write it down.

The same thing happened to me in March 2008, when without notice or desire or even an understanding of what was coming, I began to receive The 33 Lessons.

I just sat down one day, and Constance, a spirit guide who was new to me, began talking.

Out of the blue. Without warning.

And there I was on the other end, willing and able to act as scribe, recorder, and secretary for the spiritual realm.

In my research, I have come across many other folks who are receivers, and I expect we'll see this type of channeling become quite common in the coming decades. It's a part of what's happening in our growth and evolution as humans. Just as the Spiritualists received messages from the departed long ago, we now receive messages from spirit guides, angels, and other Divine beings. As we progress as a people (and even though it seems like progress is slow, evolution *is* happening), our channel to the Divine is opening, and messages are beginning to come through loud and clear.

Not just to one person, or a few, but to anyone who wishes to receive.

The Divine is now presenting itself to us in a clear and understandable way, in this time and in this culture. Not through a special priest, preacher, mystic, shaman, or guru. Not in words so cryptic no one can understand them. But in messages that can be received by anyone and can be easily understood by anyone within the container of our culture.

## We Don't Need No Stinkin' Leeches (Or Do We?)

Another way of thinking about this? Around the time of the Spiritualist movement, there were lots of bizarre medical cures. How about covering your body with leeches for bloodletting? It's a treatment most of us wouldn't request today, because it seems hopelessly old-fashioned, barbaric, not covered by health insurance—and mostly, because we've discovered new, better ways of doing things. But back to those leeches again? Today, they're used in microsurgery, to precisely drain blood from wounded sites.

In channeling, as in bloodletting, what goes around comes around. As we move forward, we perfect old-fashioned techniques, or learn new ones.

We no longer require crystal balls or Ouija boards. We don't need our Divine guidance preapproved by specialists, the way church leaders did centuries ago. Today, each of us can receive Divine guidance on our own.

## We Receive What We Need for This Time and Age

For example, in The 33 Lessons, you'll notice that the language of the Lessons is fairly simple. It's not completely modern—it makes me think that Constance and the others were from another time. But the words aren't difficult to understand. The message is clear. It's current. It's for people who exist in the world Now.

Three thousand years ago (give or take) when the Bible was first being written, it sounded completely different. In fifty, one hundred, or five hundred years, what the Divine brings to us will have a different form, sound, language entirely.

As we evolve, the look and feel of what we receive will change.

Moses received messages on stone tablets. Rumi waited for poetry to capture his soul. Neale Donald Walsch had a simple conversation with God one day, in plainspoken English.

If we are truly open to channel the Divine, guidance will come exactly as we need it, in a language we can understand.

# 6

# Get Your Channel Clear, or Can You Hear Me Now?

If you want to receive through channeling and channeled writing, the most important thing you can do is *get your channel clear*.

Not all messages come to us clearly when we channel. Sometimes there's static on the line that makes it more difficult to understand what we are receiving. In some cases, the static comes from the other side and may be caused by interfering spirits and entities. In other cases, the static comes from you.

## Interfering Spirits

A while back, I studied with Debra Lynne Katz, author of *You Are Psychic*, *Extraordinary Psychic*, and *Freeing the Genie Within* and a renowned psychic who teaches *clairvoyance*, the art of seeing psychically. Before I'd worked with Debra, my *clairaudient* (psychic hearing) and *clairsentient* (psychic feeling) skills were fully developed, but I hadn't had much luck with clairvoyance, or "seeing the movies in my head" as they say.

During one training session, we were working with a third party on a conference call. It's common to do readings via phone, and my task for this session was to do a clairvoyant reading of another woman—we'll call her Kristin. Debra was on one line, I was on another, and

Kristin was on a third line. Debra and I had already worked via conference call a few times before and the phone line had always been clear—good volume levels, easy to hear, no disconnections, no hisses, snaps, crackles, or pops.

But during Kristin's reading, my phone went crazy! Static crackled on the line, volume levels went in and out, and I kept thinking we'd get disconnected. Even more bizarre, I could actually *feel* the electricity running from the phone into my hand—there was so much energy zapping my phone, I thought it might explode right then and there!

This went on for several minutes as the three of us valiantly tried to proceed, then the connection went dead. Suspecting there might be some spirit interference, we reconnected and continued—yet the same static problems kept crackling. It wasn't until midway through the reading that I clairvoyantly "saw" the problem Kristen was having with a relative who had great influence and control over her life.

It's almost as if that person, even from a distance and with no awareness of the reading, was waiting to be mentioned—and she had something to add to the conversation. In fact, the moment I relayed this relative's message to Kristin, the crackling stopped. Even though this person was far away, she was still energetically interfering with our phone connection—just as she was interfering in Kristin's life.

It's important to remember this, because spirit energy, even the energy of people who are still very much alive, can play havoc when you are trying to receive messages. If you're having any electrical-type interference when you are receiving, this is probably the case.

When you're doing channeled writing (which we'll get to soon), the signs are easy to spot. If your laptop starts blinking and freezing and crashing, first

1. save your work! and

2. consider that you've got a case of pesky spirits who have something to say (or are trying to block something they don't want you to hear).

# When the Interference Is You

In order to act as a receiver, you need a clear channel. While you can't do too much about spirit interference, you do have control over how clear you keep the channel that is *you*.

For example: which would you rather listen to—an old transistor radio you picked up at a garage sale for two dollars, or a state-of-the-art Bose system that emits layers of lavish music, an infusion of sound so sweet and pure it make the hair on your arms stand up?

Of course, you want the Bose!

The thing is, *you* are the receiving system. You can choose to be a junky old transistor or you can be the state-of-the-art system.

How? By how you treat your body.

## Body Supports Spirit

As every yogi, health nut, or fitness aficionado knows, body supports spirit. If you eat nutritious food, if you exercise regularly, spend time in nature, if you drink water and get lots of sleep, you're going to be healthy, you're going to reduce the chance of depression and other mental health issues, and you're going to be a happier person.

Plus, you'll look better in your bathing suit, and that's always fun.

Thus, for those of you who want to receive clearly, taking care of your body in the most simple, basic ways is important.

## Substances Create Static

What kills a clear channel faster than yanking the Evereadys out of a transistor? Here's the short list:

- drugs, alcohol, and tobacco
- mental health drugs and other medications
- excessive herbs and supplements
- excessive caffeine or "energy" drinks
- junk food

- excessive food/overeating in general
- lack of food/excessive dieting

We're not talking about a glass of wine at Chez Lulu's or a beer on the deck with friends. We're not talking about skipping your heart medication, or whatever it is that you need to maintain your health. I doubt very much that chomping down a cheeseburger and fries on occasion is going to matter (unless you're a vegetarian).

But if you have addictions or use any of the above substances to excess, you're going to have more trouble receiving.

This isn't my law. It's just how it works.

This isn't about morality, either. It isn't about saying these things are wrong or right or making any judgment about substances in general. All we're talking about is how you can receive more clearly.

The trouble with substances and such is that they can make you sluggish. They can make your brain cloudy and cranky and fuzzy. Or, in the case of stimulants, they can make you wired up and jumpy.

Cloudy? Hyped up? Head too far in either of those directions, and you're going to have trouble receiving.

To clarify further—anyone over thirty reading this book had a hangover recently? (I say thirty, because that's usually when folks really realize that drinking too much incapacitates you the next day— queasy stomach, pounding headache, aversion to bright lights, etc.)

It's hard enough to slug down a cup of coffee and get to work on time with this kind of body/brain problem. But trying to go into a light meditative trance and receive Divine messages from your spirit guides?

I don't think so.

## The Problem with Mood Elevators

Lots of people use mood elevators prescribed by their physician. This is endemic to our culture right now; there are traces of Prozac and other mental health drugs already showing up in our water systems, for Pete's sake! Between 1994 and 1998, and also between 1999 and 2002, the percentage of American adults using antidepressants tripled, according a report compiled by the National Center for Health Statistics.[2]

Again, I'm not for or against mental health drugs per se. (Certainly, the jury's still out on why we need them, but I'd suspect it's because our culture is so disconnected from the Divine.) The thing to understand is that mood elevators cause changes in the way your brain works, and this can interfere with your ability to channel. I won't pretend to know what each drug does or doesn't do, but yes, they do have an effect.

If you are on a constant stream of uppers and downers and evener-outers, then channeling might not work for you. And if you've really flattened yourself into a state of numbness, channeling just can't come through. For whatever reason, and no matter how much these drugs help you get through your day, they tend to turn off the channeling power button.

As for illegal drugs—same deal. I include this category, because let's get real: even if illegal drugs are not something you're personally very aware of, they are very widely used. According to the National Household Survey on Drug Use and Health, 45 percent of Americans over age twelve have used them.[3] Drugs that are considered more hardcore, such as cocaine, meth, rave drugs and so forth? Thousands of people use these also.

These are just the facts, ma'am. And these things can make it hard to channel.

---

2 National Center for Health Statistics, 2008.
3 National Household Survey on Drug Use and Health, 2008.

*But Ram Dass Did It . . .*

Some drugs such as peyote have been used by shamans to open con-sciousness. Ram Dass is famous for using LSD back in the day and writing *Be Here Now* based in part on his experiences. Ram Dass openly admits and writes about using these consciousness-altering drugs—and certainly, his book is a brilliant, enormous work, and if you haven't read it you should put this book down right now and go find yourself a copy.

However, not everyone is Ram Dass.

While these kinds of drugs have been used successfully by some people to open consciousness, in my opinion, you don't need 'em.

After all, it's not hard to receive. But if you're busy seeing dancing leprechauns or imagining the walls of your living room melting like butter as you sit there waiting to hear from your spirit guides—yes, you can get a bit distracted.

If you want to channel easily, come to the process with a clear head. Your results will be better; you will receive messages faster and with less strain. And you will understand how to move forward to the next step in your life with the messages you receive.

## To Sleep, Perchance to Dream

Nobody sleeps any more! According to Consumer Reports National Research Center, 44 percent of Americans surveyed said they had trouble falling asleep, difficulty staying asleep, or woke up too early. In fact, the problem's so severe, one in five people take prescription or over-the-counter sleep medicines at least once a week.[4]

Yet, deep sleep is crucial for our bodies and our souls. For one thing, we do a lot of important dreamwork when we sleep. Many of us even *astral project*, which means we travel to other places while we sleep—our body is happily hogging all the covers, while our spirit is

---

4 Consumer Reports National Research Center, September 2008; National Insti-tute of Health, 2008.

traveling to exotic places like Shangri-La or Atlantis or the Indiana Jones Adventure ride at Disneyland.

Some people don't know they astral project—they just remember the clearest "dreams" about places they visited during the night. If you've every done any past-life work, you'll understand how easy it is to send your spirit off to explore other times and places while your body remains in the chair. When you astral project while dreaming, it usually happens without any intent on your part—it's just how we're designed.

Of course, dreaming doesn't always result in a crucial psychic revelation; sometimes just your subconscious working things out—a sort of patchwork puzzle of that Owen Wilson movie you just saw, that pizza you ate right before bed, the recently received information that your kid needs a costume for the school play (yes, by tomorrow), and you end up dreaming about a kid in a pizza suit on a train to Darjeeling.

No matter how silly or bizarre your dreams are, it's important to have them. If you're not sleeping regularly or enough, you're going to have trouble receiving. If you're taking sleeping pills to get to sleep and you find these affect your ability to dream, they're also going to affect your ability to channel.

### Welcome to the ZZZZZ Zone

Even if you're not a heavy sleeper, you sleep away much of your life. Snoozing a healthy eight hours per night? Why, that's one third of your twenty-four-hour day. Another way to look at it? That's one third of your life! Sleep is a time of great healing and rejuvenation, and it's where we do a lot of our soul work.

But aside from the great benefits of sleep, catching enough zzzzz's is a purely practical manner for those who want to channel.

Why? Because if you don't get enough sleep, you're probably going to drift off during receiving.

If you're overtired, exhausted, and sleep deprived, it's really hard to stay in an alert, light trance state while you receive. In workshops, whenever the trance state is introduced, you'll see it again and again—the head bobs, the body droops, and suddenly the room is filled with the gentle (or not so gentle) snoring of the sleep-deprived participant. An entire workshop afternoon can go by as the sleeper slumbers peacefully on, waking up only during the concluding comments, rubbing his eyes and muttering, "Did I miss something?"

If you need sleep, your body will grab it when the chance occurs—and you'll miss out on receiving. So if you're planning a channeling session, get to bed early the night before or take a catnap beforehand.

## The Need for Downtime

If you are working full time, or taking care of a family, or if you are doing what so many people do nowadays, working full time *and* taking care of a family, you are insanely busy.

Repeat after me: this is insanity.

We've entered an age of distraction, an era in which we're not only multitasking, we're multitasking while driving to seven places in one hour! I know toddlers with older siblings involved in this sport and that dance lesson, and these fresh, inquisitive, beautiful little souls spend multiple hours of their young lives each day strapped into their car seat in the back of the family van as Mom chauffeurs everyone around.

A large chunk of their young lives is being spent looking at the back of Mom's headrest.

Repeat after me (yes, one more time!): this is insanity.

It's not good for Baby. It's definitely not good for Mom. And the family as a whole suffers because everything is so locked into the stress of *go, go, go!*

Even if you aren't chauffeuring a bunch of kids to activities, chances are you're busy. Maybe you're one of the "sandwich generation," and are taking care of both older and younger family members. Maybe you're a workaholic, or your work is very intense. Perhaps you need to work two or even three jobs to support yourself. Maybe you're just overscheduled, running from one distraction to the next. Maybe you're addicted to distraction, afraid of what might happen—how you might feel—if you stop.

Whatever your situation, when you're overly busy and stressed, it's hard to channel.

When you are operating at this level of adrenal overdrive, it's also hard to settle down at night, which is why so many of us watch TV as a way of winding down before bed. Of course, TV doesn't relax you—it actually provides further stimulus. And after you've stayed up too late, your poor body is left with just a few hours of sleep to heal itself during sleep. Usually, that's not enough.

The antidote to this kind of crazy scheduling is *downtime*. What's downtime? Think of everything your mother ever told you was "lazy," or your sixth grade teacher called "daydreaming." Think of Robert Fulghum in *All I Really Need to Know I Learned in Kindergarten*, promoting the benefits of naptime.

This is downtime, and for anyone who wants to channel, it is essential.

Ideally, you'd have entire days of doing nothing—days where you could wander around the house without a schedule or a plan or chores to do—in fact, you might even get bored.

Now, most people don't have free time in those vast increments. But you can definitely can grab an hour, even a half hour, and go to a park or out in nature, and just sit and *be*. Don't bring a book, don't play your iPod, don't check your BlackBerry. Just sit, let the wind blow on your face, watch the leaves on the trees rustle and sway.

Or, you can take a long, hot bath. (This is especially good for those of you with young kids, where some days you literally have to lock yourself in the bathroom to get some alone time. I know this, because

I Have Been There.) Take a soak, and just sit there until the bubbles dissipate. Let your mind float. Be serene.

Tubbing not your style? Then lie on the sofa, the way you did when you were a teen. Don't sit properly—sprawl. Turn upside down and stare at the ceiling, and don't immediately chastise yourself for the cobwebs that need to be dusted. Just stare into space, and let your mind drift. Don't think about what you should do, or what you have to do, or where you need to be. Don't have your journal ready, don't read a book, don't make a to-do list, put the scrapbooking away. Simply let your mind drift along, like a boat cut free on a small, gentle pond.

If you question whether you are doing downtime "right," simply ask yourself, "Did I get anything done?" If you accomplished anything except drifting thoughts, you're working too hard!

If you question whether you deserve downtime when you have so much to do, there is only one answer: you not only deserve downtime, you require it.

So go ahead. Goof off. Sprawl. Laze.

Go back to the time you were a kid, and spent the entire afternoon lying in the sweet grass staring at the sky.

If you never did this as a kid, do it now.

How long is long enough? When you feel time has actually shifted—when you can sit on a sofa for an hour doing absolutely nothing and feel like you've been there five minutes, then you've got the hang of downtime.

Downtime may sound silly, but it unlocks the part of your brain you will need for channeling. (As an added benefit, it also unlocks the part of your brain you need for creative thinking and problem solving.) If you want to channel clearly, you will need frequent downtime.

## The Need for Exercise

I watch runners loping along the road with envy, because I am not of their ilk. Oh sure, I have the fantasy: there's me, sprinting along like a gazelle, hair flying in the breeze, eating up the miles with my long-legged, endorphin-fueled stride, pure poetry in motion.

However, my actual ability to run is more along the lines of:

*Trot, trot, trot. Spend five minutes doubled over track, sucking air, while pretending to look at small bug on ground. Trot, trot. Stop ten minutes for pulled hamstring, while pretending to do important warm-up stretch. Trot. Stop. Hobble off track, pretending nothing. Get icepack, get ibuprofen, swear off running forever.*

As you might have guessed, I am not a runner.

Hmmmm. I'm also not a tennis player, golfer, yoga practitioner, hiker, soccer player, skydiver, bowler, rock climber, gym-machine user, skier, or skater.

However, I do love to dance and swim. I also like to boogie board, kayak on nary-a-ripple rivers, and ride my bike in a leisurely, ambling kind of way. What's more, this is just fine.

Having a physical life in which you *live in your body* is conducive to receiving. But you don't have to be a marathoner, ice climber, or star athlete to be physical. However, if you don't exercise at all, your body will get all crunchy and crusty—think of poor Gregor Samsa turning into a cockroach in Franz Kafka's *The Metamorphosis*. If you're hunched over a computer all day, and then hunched over a steering wheel in the afternoon, and then sacked out in front of the TV all night, and then lying comatose in bed—if you don't move and live as a physical person in a physical body—you can become very cockroach-like indeed.

Cockroaches are not normally good channels.

Thus, find something you like to do—rollerblading, ping-pong playing, bungee jumping—it doesn't matter what. Do it as often as you can, and notice how much better you feel. Remember: body supports spirit. Simply living in your body helps you tune into channeling more easily.

## The Need for Nature

I am extraordinarily blessed to live right in the middle of a community of ancient trees. My house is literally surrounded by them. Some days, when I am feeling stressed from deadlines and responsibilities and the Divine seems like a distant dream, I will head out and sit among these lovely Pacific Northwest beings, and *connect* with them. I simply close my eyes, take a deep breath, and the instantaneous peace that comes is truly remarkable—suddenly I feel the breeze on my cheek, hear the trees sing in the air, and become aware that these particular old firs and maples and oaks and yews were standing here long before me and will be here long after I am gone.

So many of us live so much of our lives inside—shuffling from car to school to office to car to home—that we don't even get a chance to see the seasons change. The new buds of spring, the heady mown-grass scent of summer, the exhilarating dry-leaf crispness of fall, the blustery drama of winter; we miss everything when we're stuck inside our air-conditioned, climate-controlled boxes.

The truth is, the more you can get outside in nature, the better you will be able to receive. Even nature that is not very natural—a crowded city park, an outdoor soccer field, a walk in suburbia—allows us a glimpse of earth and open sky.

This is important, because nature *opens* us. All nature—from trees, plants, and sky to water, earth, and animal—is organic, living, and filled entirely with the Divine. The more time we spend in nature, even the smallest patch, the more we are opened. And when we spend time in wilderness, we can become so open we feel awe.

# 7

## What to Expect When You're Channeling

You wouldn't parachute before you knew how to pull the ripcord, would you?

Of course you wouldn't.

That's why we're going to start with channeling first, and then move on to channeled writing once you have some skills firmly under your belt.

For those of you who are overachievers, a word of caution: if you skip ahead to the channeled writing section now, without doing the groundwork that's required, you're going to be frustrated, and you're not going to receive as clearly.

Sorry. That's just how it works.

Of course, you've already been *in the field* during your warm-up channeling. But once you go in deeper, your brain (and your emotions) will need a few sessions to adapt to the experience before you start adding in laptops and computers and pens and paper and journaling and manifesting. Please, allow yourself this time.

# Who You Might Hear From

Since most people have similar types of experiences when channeling, it's good to know some of these options beforehand, so you can recognize them if they start happening to you (and they may have already happened to you during the warm-up session). First, when you channel for the Highest Good, different types of spirit entities may arrive to you. These may include:

- spirit guides who bring you messages
- angels who bring you messages
- spiritual entities such as Esther Hick's Abraham, who speak *through* you
- people who have passed on before, such as ancestors and dead relatives
- people who've passed on whom you don't know
- visions and premonitions
- songs or music, either that you hear or that is channeled through you
- healing energies that arrive into or move through your body
- the universe, the cosmos, the Source—the ineffable bliss of the Divine.

It's a lot to take in all at once, so let's go over them in detail.

## SPIRIT GUIDES

These are ascended beings. Some of you will have the same spirit guides with you throughout your life. Others might have spirit guides who change over time. My primary spirit guide is Hajam, who's signed on with me for life—he's my permanent Camp Buddy in the Cosmos. Other spirit guides seem to come and go. For example, some years back I had a spirit guide named Susan—she was extremely tall, almost elongated, wore a sort of robe thing, and had long, dark hair. She was very intense and authoritative, and I must admit I was a bit frightened of her. I've also had a sweet-as-pie older lady with a cotton-ball puff of white hair named Betty Ann. Recently, I've worked with Constance, Miriam, and Gabriel, who dictated The 33 Lessons. However, all three made it clear to me that they weren't my personal spirit guides per se—they were just there to dictate The Lessons.

I frequently see Hajam; as I mentioned earlier, he's a slight, bald Indian or Asian man. He's usually wearing baggy shorts, and his legs are bare. He has a big, smiling face. I don't see him physically in the room with me; I see him in my mind's eye, exactly the way you'd see a movie in your head, with full sound, color, and action. He's both demanding and sympathetic—he gets in my face when I am not getting the message clearly and marches around using hand signals to make his point more clearly!

Just last week, I received a visitation from an extremely tall, elongated being whose name was Raegulf or Ragnar or something like that. He appeared at my left shoulder and didn't say anything, but simply let his presence be known as if in introduction. I have the distinct feeling I'll be hearing more from him the next time I go into the field.

### The Purpose of Spirit Guides

Spirit guides are here to help you on your life path. They are here to help you:

- figure out your life's purpose,
- make decisions when you are confused,
- work through issues you need to work through,
- help you to the next spiritual level,
- assist you with every aspect of your soul growth,
- help you with the practicalities of life, and
- be a sustaining source of comfort and Divine bliss.

However, spirit guides are not Santa Claus. They don't go around doling out new cars and winning lottery tickets—unless, of course, these are directly related to your soul growth.

Spirit guides aren't God—but then again, they're not *not* God. They're a part of God, just as you and I are. What spirit guides do is *make it easier for us to understand the Divine*. For example, you wouldn't give a toddler a book called *An Existential Philosophy of Universal Love*, now would you? No, you'd give your toddler a cozy teddy bear, and she'd hug it and learn how to love right there on the spot.

In the same way, spirit guides teach you in the ways you learn fastest—they meet you where you are. And just like a teddy bear, they love and comfort you, and they'll never let you down.

Some people never meet their spirit guides, and this is okay. Some people have trouble believing in spirit guides; this is fine, too! There are many ways to receive Divine guidance; spirit guides are just one of them.

### Discovering Your Spirit Guide's Name

Want to know your spirit guide's name? Ask! Plus, go ahead and ask anything else you're curious about: "Where'd you come from?" "Have we met before?" "What is your purpose?" and so on. If it's something you need to know, they'll tell you.

When I first met Hajam, I asked him his name repeatedly, but because I'd never heard that name before, I couldn't understand what he was saying. If this happens to you, ask your spirit to *write* their name for you. They'll actually write it in letters you can read in your mind's eye. It's wonderful to know your spirit guide's name! This is precious information, and it's comforting to have.

## Angels

So many people have done such beautiful work on angels! I've studied author Doreen Virtue so many times, amazed at how she teaches people to see angels through her writings and in her workshops. Sophy Burnham is another renowned author who gives us a glimpse of the grace of these Holy Beings.

Angels have been with us since humankind began. Great works of art often show angels revealing themselves to humans, guardian angels protecting children, or powerful angels battling the forces of evil.

Many people see angels all the time!

Well, guess what? I must confess that I'd *never* seen an angel (and not for lack of trying!) until I received The 33 Lessons. During one of the early sessions, Constance (a spirit guide) had told me that another would arrive, "and he is mighty." When Gabriel arrived, I was terrified! I mean, Gabriel! We're talking archangels here!

Yet, the Gabriel who arrived to me was not an angel with big wings and blazing trumpets, halo the size of a dinner plate and so forth. This Divine angel was a young being with curly reddish-brown hair and a sweet smile. He was the most gentle, beautiful soul—infinitely patient and kind. He sat beside me with such stillness, it was pure bliss to be in his presence and to receive his teachings.

Since that time, I have frequently seen angels who appear in human form—mysterious "people" who suddenly arrived when grace was needed, and the next time I looked, they were gone. Poof. Vanished. I see these kinds of angels all the time.

Your angels can take many forms. Just as with spirit guides, don't expect them to look or act a certain way.

Angels do basically the same job as spirit guides—help you in your soul growth. They are also active helpers and protectors (whereas spirit guides are more advisory) and may be called on for help at any time, in any situation. If you are in trouble, need help, or feel afraid, simply ask your angels to come to you, and they will be there instantly.

I have taught this tool to my youngest daughter, and she finds comfort in knowing that her angels are always near.

## Vocalized Channeling

If you should feel your throat start to gurgle and sounds coming out of your mouth, you may be channeling another entity through your body. This is the type of channeling that Esther Hicks does when she channels the entity known as Abraham, or that other channelers do when they receive through their voice.

Does this happen to a lot of people? I'd say the answer is: nobody knows yet. It's certainly very rare now, but as more and more people start to use channeling as a tool for spiritual growth, we'll see if this ability becomes more widespread.

Is vocalized channeling "fancier" or better than other methods? No, it's not. It's just another method, that's all.

If this type of vocalized channeling is happening to you, arrange to have a recording device on hand, or a friend who will transcribe what you say. Many of those who channel this way are unaware of what happens when the other entity "steps in" to use their voice, so it's good to have some method of recording.

Finally, this type of channeling isn't usually meant as tool for your own personal Divine guidance; most often these vocalized teachings are provided as spiritual teachings.

## Departed Souls

If you'll recall, most of the Spiritualism movement at the turn of the century focused on connection with departed souls—people who'd recently died. In general, messages from departed souls are a tool to help those who are grieving.

Departed souls are not yet ascended—they're stuck between their old lives on earth and their new lives in the next realm. But sometimes they hang around for a while, either unable to let go and move on, or because they have leftover business to attend to.

If you should meet a departed soul while channeling, attempt to pass on its message to the proper recipient. On the other hand, if you run across a departed soul that seems mischievous, tricky, bewildered, grasping, needy, or belligerent, simply and firmly *ask them to leave.*

Say "skedaddle" or "get out" or "be gone."

Shout "go home!" or "party's over!" the way you might yell at a scruffy stray dog who's slunk into your yard. You're not afraid. You're not being mean. You're just firm. These spirits are very low types of energy, and they're no match for you channeling the Divine.

Not sure when a spirit's a low-life? Trust your instincts. You're going to know immediately whether or not the spirits you meet are good or bad forces. If you get hassled by some punk spirit guides, just shoo them away—firmly, confidently, and *loudly.* They'll get the message and back off.

Now, we've all seen movies where bad spirits cause your head to spin around backwards, but I think that's a case of film directors having overactive imaginations. That certainly hasn't been my experience; I've had almost zero trouble with these lower spirits.

A few months ago, I noticed a pesky spirit hanging around the basement of my house—I think it was the ghost of a man who'd lived there before. I told him he didn't live there any more and asked him to leave, and he did.

Another time, a low-life spirit was interfering with the sound system at the recording studio we use. I'd been working all morning with our engineer, and the equipment had been going crazy! We hadn't lost any files yet, but the system, which is normally flawless, had crashed repeatedly. Suddenly, I felt something over my shoulder. I turned fast, and there it was—a blob of dark spirit energy, hanging out by the window.

"Who was here yesterday?" I asked the engineer, and he mentioned a singer/songwriter I know, a man who's totally in flow.

Wasn't him.

"Anyone else?"

"Yeah, a guy who plays in his band."

"What's his vibe?" I asked, carefully keeping my eye on the dark cluster of energies in the corner.

"Not good," he said mildly.

Those two words said it all.

"Let's get rid of it," I said, and as if on cue, we swiveled in our chairs and yelled, "Get out of here!" at the top of our lungs.

Poof. Spirit vanished. Bad vibe gone. And the recording equipment? It worked perfectly the rest of the day.

If you run into lower spirits, simply demand that they leave, and remember: they are no match for you connected to the Divine.

## Scents and Sounds

This category of receiving is most often picked up by those of you who are clairsentient, or have psychic feelings. For example, if your grandfather smoked cigars, you might smell a strong odor of cigar smoke when he is trying to contact you. Sometimes entities use the senses as a shortcut to help you understand quickly who is trying to contact you—e.g., if it's cigar smoke, it's Grandpa.

You might also hear specific sounds, such as music or a song playing that has special meaning for you. Simply pay attention to what you receive in this way, and you will find that its significance is either clear to you immediately or will become clear to you very soon.

# 8

⌒

# What Channeling
# Sounds and Looks Like

## A Different Way of Hearing

The way you hear when you're channeling isn't the same way you hear in your everyday life. It's not as direct. A car honk that you hear on the street is blaring, loud, jarring. A car honk that you hear when you are channeling may be muffled or distant—it's the same sound, but it's harder to hear.

Sometimes, you just *sense* the sound, if that makes any sense. In other words, *you hear it in your mind.* To be even more specific, for most people, channeling voices sounds *like your own voice in your head.* Some people call this the voice of your Higher Self or the Divine Self—the part of us that is God.

It is key that you understand that receiving may not sound like golden angels trumpeting at you from across the room! It might . . . but most people simply hear a voice that comes into one ear, or an inner voice, or have the feeling that a thought is being impressed upon their mind. These are all ways of receiving.

Remember, I work experientially—that is, I teach only what I have experienced firsthand. My experience is that when I channel messages from spirit guides, they don't sound like me. They have accents, different speech patterns, or they use different words than are in my normal vocabulary. I hear them in my head, but it's definitely not my own voice.

Plus, the content of what I hear is different from my inner thoughts. For example, my own inner voice tends to do a lot of panicking about what deadlines I need to meet, how much weight I need to lose, what bills I need pay, and so forth.

Pretty boring stuff.

Basically, my spirit guides would never stoop to worrying about something so earthly as a deadline! They'd say: "We love you." "You're doing great." "All things will be done in the time you need," and with that, send me a big wave of Divine bliss that is infinitely comforting.

## A Voice In One Ear

When doing channeled writing, I hear a voice specifically in one ear, usually my right ear, almost as if the spirit guide is sitting on that side of me. For example, when I channeled The 33 Lessons, Constance always appeared (in my mind's eye) directly in front of me, not as close as Hajam does, but about five feet away. Her voice came into my right ear. Sometimes her voice would sound distant. When this happened, I sat still, with my eyes closed, and said aloud, "I can't hear you," or "I'm having trouble hearing," and then waited. I never experience crackling or any other technological interference, the way we have trouble with our phones—instead, it was as if Constance was having trouble maintaining communication, or for some reason my window was not fully open.

## Keeping Your Window Open

Twice in my channeled writings (but four years apart), I was given the example of communicating through *windows*—once in The Truths, and later in The 33 Lessons. In the first case, the example was given with an onion; later on, the same lesson was given using an orange. As you can see, these words are similar, and might even sound similar: onion, orange. But the lesson was identical—the idea of a sphere within a sphere within a sphere. Picture an onion with its many peelable inner layers, and you've got the concept.

Within each layer, Constance said, there's an active area called a portal or window. When the top layer is aligned with the layer beneath it or the layer above it, these windows also become aligned. This is where communication between you and Spirit happens.

The layers are the different realms: our realm here on earth, the realm of the newly departed, the realm of spirit guides and angels, and so forth. I do not claim to know if the layers are indeed round, like an onion, or horizontal, or if they even have shape at all—this was just the example given to me, to help understand the concept of windows.

Any time you are communicating with another realm, at least two windows must be open: yours and theirs.

It's possible that *all the windows in every single layer* could be opened at once! I suspect this is what happens with angels, the ascended, and others in sublime states of soul growth who are able to communicate across many realms.

This means that, during the channeling of The 33 Lessons, two things had to happen:

1. Constance had to make herself known to me, and

2. I had to agree to channel.

In other words, we both needed to open our windows in order to communicate. If Constance calls me all day long, but I don't open my window, we can't communicate.

And vice versa.

Another way to look at it? It's like your cell phone. You can make the call, but somebody has to pick up. Both connections have to be open.

Of course, even if both windows are open, it can be hard to receive. We all know how difficult and confusing it can be to communicate with someone who doesn't speak the same language. Now, imagine trying to communicate with an entity from another realm. You say onion, I say orange—no wonder it can be hard to hear!

## Warnings, Flashes, and Hits

Frequently, I receive short, one- or two-word messages in my ear. These happen when I'm going about my regular day—when I'm not in trance or a state of receiving.

These are often warnings or commands, and I receive them as sharp, abrupt words, such as "Move now!" or "Get away!"

It took me a long time to learn this, but when these urgent messages come to you, I strongly advise you to:

1. Pay attention, and

2. Do what they say!

Don't ask why! Don't ask questions! Don't dilly-dally! Simply follow this guidance immediately—it comes to you for your protection and safety.

Last summer, for example, I received a warning as I was leaving the house. "Check the stove!" a voice said, right in my ear. The words were strong and forceful, and I paid immediate attention. I raced back into the house and to my shock, found that the gas on the stove had been left on, and highly explosive gas was filling the kitchen and living room! Quickly I turned the gas off, then wrenched open doors and windows, and *got out*! The whole family stayed outside until the gas had dissipated and all danger of explosion was past. If I'd left without heeding this warning, there would have surely been a fire.

Another way of receiving these short, immediate messages is through what I call flashes or hits. It's your gut instinct on turbo-charge; you suddenly just "know" something. As you become more open to channeling in this way—through fast, sudden bursts of information—you move into a higher state of awareness, and you'll start experiencing this all the time.

Getting a flash doesn't have to be about something earth-shattering, either. Sometimes it's about silly stuff. The other day, I was talking to my teenage son about how awful it is when birds poop on your head (as you can tell, my life is exciting and dynamic!). As we were laughing about this natural phenomenon, I said brazenly, "Well, thank goodness that's never happened to me!"

Immediately, I got the flash: "Oh, but it will!" Sure enough, two days later we were on a bike ride, and a bird pooped on my head! I can't say my spirit guides didn't warn me.

## BEING WILLING TO RECEIVE

It is not important how you hear—your own voice in your head, another voice in your head, another voice in the room. What is important is that you listen.

*Being willing to receive is half the battle.*

Thus, if you are having a lot of interference because

- your own voice is chattering loudly about how weird this is, or

- you're worried that you won't receive correctly, or

- you're worried that you won't receive at all,

please let these thoughts go.

Vinn Marti, creator of Soul Motion™, teaches people how awaken their souls through dance and movement. As part of his workshops, he'll often have people stand still on the dance floor and wait for their next movement to present itself to them. The idea is to deal with the discomfort that happens when you don't know the next step to your dance—or to your life.

"Wait," Vinn advises. "Wait . . . for further instruction."

It's good advice for channeling, too. When things get unclear, simply wait . . . for further instruction. Let yourself become open and pliant to the Divine. Open your window all the way, and then open it some more. Making yourself available to receive is the most important requirement when you are channeling.

## A Different Way of Seeing

Visually, channeling can be as clear as if an entity is standing right next to you in the room. Or, you might see nothing.

Nothing!

Clairvoyance is one of the most difficult channeling skills to gain— I don't know why this is; it's just the skill most people have trouble with. Be patient, and don't worry if it doesn't happen immediately. As you practice and understand what to expect, most people are able to become clairvoyant.

### VISUAL RECEIVING

For most people, visual receiving usually progresses like this:

1. You see nothing.

2. You have a sense of something in the room with you. You may or may not be able to see it, but you know it's there. This might be a sense of lightness, a denseness of energy, flickering lights, or the sense that the energy is different, active, faster, thicker, or denser.

3. You see a spirit entity's face and body in your mind's eye, but it doesn't move much. It's more like a static image on a screen.

4. You see a symbolic picture in your mind's eye that doesn't move much. For example, a giant key, a dollar bill, a stop sign.

5. You see images moving in your mind's eye like a movie—spirit entities, other people, symbolic items. The movie may be hazy or luminous like a dream, where you can see some of it, but not all the details.

6. The moving picture in your mind's eye is easy to see, and contains both movement and sound. You can look in any direction, zoom in for a close-up, zoom out to go far away.

7. You can move freely in the moving picture in your mind's eye, from room to room and so forth. By working with this, you'll soon have the ability to travel in space while your body stays where you are (astral projection). For example, you might easily travel to Florida if you live in Oregon—even if you've never been to Florida. When you get to Florida, you can look clearly around and see where you are and all the details of that scene.

8. You see angels, spirits, and visions in the room with you—they move, you can hear them, and they appear real or nearly real.

Remember, it's not important what level of clairvoyance you achieve. I've never been able to get to step eight consistently—actually seeing angels in the room as physical entities, outside of my mind's eye. Maybe I'll be able to do that later, or maybe I won't. It's not that important.

What's important is that you are okay with what you do see.

## Images Are Symbolic

Channeling visual imagery clairvoyantly is different from channeling voices and sound, because it's symbolic. Even if you clearly see a movie playing in your mind, you have to interpret that movie.

For example, say you receive a clairvoyant message of a butler, a serving tray, and a lobster. Does this mean you should get a job in the service industry? Hire a butler? Eat seafood more often? It's unclear.

Whereas, if you clairaudiently hear a voice tell you, "That woman you're dating is a lobster; watch out for her sharp claws," it's easier to correctly interpret the message.

## How Will You Receive?

If you're like most people, you're going to channel better some ways than others. For example, some people deal primarily with spirit guides. They see them standing beside their chair; they're able to relay their messages clearly; this is their main method of connection. My friend Hollee Haas, a speaker, presenter, and psychic consultant, works effortlessly in this way.

Other channelers are expert at hearing the voices of the departed. These people are sought out by those who are grieving, and many of them talk about being compelled to give messages from the departed to living relatives and friends. The psychic Lisa Williams is an example of someone with this gift.

Some channelers have the ability of letting their own voices be used by other entities. Receiver Esther Hicks, who channels the spiritual entity Abraham, has gained world recognition for her abilities in voice channeling.

Will you start seeing spirit guides? Will you start getting messages from folks who've passed on? Will you start channeling voices? I have no idea—and you won't either, until you go into the field and try it yourself!

One thing I can assure you is that even though you may "open" to channeling faster than you might guess, you'll be ready for it when it happens. The Divine knows when you are ready, and won't provide this opening until you've reached a certain stage of soul growth—until you've learned the life lessons you need to be able to deal with this new ability.

# 9

## Channeling Is a Physical Act

When you channel, please expect to feel it in your body! You may experience temperature changes in your body from extreme heat to extreme cold. I always have a blanket or sweater handy when I am channeling, and most times, I get so cold that I lose sensation in my fingertips. Often, my teeth chatter from the chill.

It's not just the temperature changes, either. The truth is, channeling is plain physically demanding. Many times after a big episode of channeling, I will have to take a nap. While I don't normally take naps, after a session of channeling, I'll walk around like a zombie until I've caught twenty minutes of zzzzs. It just wipes me out.

Remember, channeling is allowing a Divine force to move through you—as a channel, you get out of the way and let the Divine pour through. The Divine is energy, and sometimes this energy can do weird things to your body.

One of the weirdest things I've experienced during channeling is shuddering. I don't mean little quivery-quakes or trembles—I mean big, nine-on-a-Richter-scale, rock-your-world shudders, a sensation that reminds me of the contractions of labor, right before your doctor says, "Start pushing!"

For all you ladies who've birthed some babies, you know these are some big sensations!

For me, the shuddering often starts right at the moment when I fully enter trance, when I first feel the channeled energy moving through my body.

## Physical Reactions to Channeling

My shuddering started a number of years ago, soon after I'd met my spirit guide Hajam, and started receiving The Truths. At the time, my neck was hurting, and I asked my partner—a chiropractor and gifted healer—to help.

From the moment he put his hand on the back of my neck, my body began shuddering in huge convulsions. It was as if massive electrical current was running up and down my spine—and I couldn't stop it.

I would have been embarrassed, mortified, quite happy to sink into any available hole in the ground and let the earth swallow me up—if I hadn't thought I was dying.

Did I have epilepsy?

Was I having a seizure?

I had no idea what was happening, as I lay there convulsing and contracting. The shuddering didn't hurt—but I couldn't turn it off.

This went on for a very long time. Ten minutes? Fifteen? I couldn't say how long, but it seemed like forever. And every time I thought it was over . . . it started up again.

When it finally, *finally* stopped, I took some very deep breaths, said something inane like, "Well, that was something," and he adjusted my neck.

Nowadays, shuddering is a part of my life. It happens when I meditate, and always right before I go into trance. It also happens when I listen to certain kinds of ambient music. It's the main reason I don't go to yoga class (not much fun convulsing like a fish out of water in front of twenty other people!). It happens sometimes when I am dancing, and frequently when I am being very still in nature.

I have consulted with physicians and psychics and healers, and nobody knows what it is. Some folks think it's a kundalini awakening—but c'mon, all the time? I mean, wouldn't you be awake enough after one awakening? Three different massage therapists told me it wouldn't last, that it would go away within a few months. That didn't happen.

During a recent session with an energy healer, I shuddered without stopping for almost three hours as he worked on me with Reiki and other energy techniques.

Three hours!

One psychic said it was the beginning of my channeling another entity. Another psychic told me I was channeling healing energies through my body.

Well, guess what? I still don't know what it is, and it hasn't stopped! I've decided not to worry about it. I'm grateful to receive this method of energy channeling, even if I don't understand it.

Will you start shuddering when you channel?

Who knows?

Channeling is full of surprises.

Be open, and let it happen.

## Channeling Makes You Feel

Channeling can be an enormous tool to help you along your life path—perhaps one of the most useful you will find. That said, there's something else you should know: *channeling brings up stuff.*

Now, I don't care who you are, or how perfect you look on the surface, you've got your stuff. When you're first starting to grow as a person and a soul, you deal with basic stuff. As you become more evolved, you still have stuff—it's just deeper-level stuff.

Whether you're going through a messy divorce, got fired from your job, have a weight issue, are dealing with an addiction, your kids have gone astray, you're suffering from grief, your credit cards are sky high, or you're dealing with an illness—whew. We humans go through a lot of stuff.

Channeling allows you to go very deep, and to be healed by the Divine. Along the way, however, emotions are going to happen. These might include:

- sorrow
- pain
- anger
- hatred
- regret
- grief
- compassion

- release
- relief
- forgiveness
- gratitude
- peace
- bliss
- love

As you can see, it's a full lineup of the good, the bad, and the ugly. When you first start to channel, you'll probably feel an abiding sense of peace, similar to when you pray or meditate. Mmmmm. That's nice, isn't it? But as you go deeper, a certain balancing and rearranging begins to take place, and all those emotions you've suppressed and ignored and refused to acknowledge will start bubbling to the surface.

Yuck.

As we all know, it can be uncomfortable to feel emotion, especially if you've bottled it up for a long time.

I've had channeling sessions where the tears streamed down my face the entire time, and I've been sacked out on the sofa afterward feeling deeply sad.

I've had channeling sessions where the error of my ways was revealed to me gently—and sometimes not so gently—and I've had to come to terms with all the mistakes I've made, all the pain and hurt I've caused others in my life.

And, I've had channeling sessions where my heart was opened so much it hurt—and then it opened more.

How will you feel?

## You May Feel Some Discomfort

Imagine taking a rotten tooth out of your mouth. For months that tooth has been causing nothing but trouble—it hurts and hurts. It has to be removed for you to get better, and it's really gonna hurt when it gets yanked out! Yet, once it's gone, the pain stops. Your mouth can heal.

Yes, the emotions might hurt at first, or even for a while. But after you get through them, you will become transformed, and you will find yourself reaching a state of peace, bliss, and love more and more often.

Every time you connect deeply with the Divine in this way, you receive a little bit of Divine peace, bliss, and love.

How will you know?

Well, for one thing, you'll feel better—a lot better—right away. Even if you have experienced difficult emotions, they will be tinged with a sense of Divine peace—a certain comfort of the heart.

And if you get to bliss?

If you get to bliss, there is no turning back, my friend.

## How Will You Know It's Bliss?

The signs of bliss in the body are quite easy to identify. Sometimes bliss comes as total body-mind euphoria, an ecstatic altered state, what we think of when we hear the phrase "blissed out." Other times, bliss is a smaller wave of yummy, feel-good-style happiness. Here, fifteen signs you're there:

**Fifteen Signs of Bliss**

1. Your jaws are relaxed; you can easily smile. You may have trouble NOT smiling!

2. You laugh freely. In fact, you may find yourself laughing without any reason.

3. It's easy to close your eyes, yet you are not sleepy.

4. Your body may tingle or vibrate, especially down your spine, neck, or head.

5. You have a feeling of expansiveness in the chest.

6. You have a feeling of lightness or floating; there is no sensation of heaviness.

7. You feel deeply relaxed, yet highly alert.

8. Your heart feels at peace.

9. You feel safe in the environment you are in, no matter where this is.

10. You feel expanded in your connection to the world and to the space around you.

11. You feel a rush that is not an adrenal rush, but a euphoric rush.

12. You don't feel physical pain, or your pain is lifted or blocked.

13. You feel a sense of Divine grace, of being in the presence of the universal Divine.

14. You experience a state of altered consciousness, an ecstatic state.

15. You may experience a state of suspended or contracted time; you understand the illusion of time.

Bliss may last for a moment, or it may last for a lifetime. It may descend upon you even when it's not sought out or expected. Extreme experiences of ecstatic bliss may result in an altered state that changes a person forever.

All the great mystics and spiritual teachers, such as Jesus, Buddha, and Mohammed, felt bliss all the time. These beings existed in a state of never-ending bliss.

Infants, children, the elderly, the mentally disabled, and those who have been enlightened by great sacrifice or pain may also exist primarily in a state of bliss.

## How Will You Open?

I didn't start channeling until 2004, when I first met my spirit guide, Hajam. In fact, I didn't even know what channeling was when I first did it.

In hindsight, I see that I had my abilities from childhood, I just hadn't used them yet. As early as the fourth grade, I was checking out stacks of books on religion, spirituality, and the paranormal from the local library. It didn't seem weird to me—it just sort of made sense, as if it was something I already knew.

I conducted mini séances in my bedroom (nobody showed up!). I read up on the occult, and found it creeped me out. I studied the paranormal, and found it fascinating. I attempted to bend spoons with my mind (it never worked), levitate myself (that didn't work either), and read minds (that worked!). I played with a Ouija board once or twice but stopped—that also felt creepy. I vividly recall being transfixed by the cathedrals we visited in Europe (I lived there during part of my childhood), and being in awe of the deep, ancient energy there. I also remember walking through cemeteries on Memorial Day and not being a bit afraid. It felt like a big party going on, all of the spirits coming out to say hello to their visiting relatives.

I don't know what happened, but sometime in my teens, after an entire childhood of being open, I shut down. I didn't allow this part of myself to be revealed. I shut down, and tried very hard to fit in and be normal.

Whatever "normal" is.

Why did I stop letting myself be "open"? I don't know. Life has many lessons to teach us, and perhaps it was time for me to focus on more earth-based skills, like how to get through high school and college, get a job, pay the rent, and later, when I was a new mother, what to do when your baby has a fever of 104. In any case, I shut down. By the time I was in my late thirties, I'd missed everything that had happened in the field of human spiritual development those past twenty years. Seth? A *Course in Miracles*? Krishnamurti? Transcendental Meditation? And so on, and so on? Never heard of any of it.

What's more, *I no longer believed*. Any mention of spirit guides, and I'd scoff openly. No one could convince me that channeling wasn't fake. I couldn't stand meditation—my mind raced around like a cat chasing a laser pointer. I refused to set foot inside a yoga class. To my mind, kundalini was some kind of pasta, and chakras were a joke. I didn't pray. I didn't meditate. I didn't connect.

As you might imagine, these were not my best years.

I'm sure that during those decades of dead zone, my spirit guides (Hajam especially) were making themselves known as loudly as they could. But I wasn't listening. I ignored them, time after time, until finally, the Divine had to interfere.

How? Well, in the course of three years:

I had a near-death experience.

My dad died.

I got divorced.

I'm not going to go into all the details of those experiences here, but these three inarguably rotten things happened to me, one after another, as a direct result of Divine intervention because I needed to "open." Other people were involved in these experiences, and I do not pretend to have any idea what the Divine had in store for them; we are all on our own path. What I needed, however, was to wake up and pay attention. And when I finally opened, I had a half a lifetime of catching up to do.

The funny thing is, as soon as I was awake, as soon as I experienced a direct connection with the Divine, everything started to happen at a dizzying rate. It seemed like each time I figured out one step on my life's path, the next step immediately presented itself, and after that, the next—like being on a turbo-charged escalator at the mall.

Once I got it—once I understood that there was no road worth traveling other than the path directed by the Divine—my life started to happen with amazing speed and beauty.

This is how it will work for you, too.

## You Will Open In Different Ways

Writing was the first channeling method that opened for me. Looking back, I believe that I was sent this gift first because writing is in my genetic code: my grandfather was a Chicago journalist, my father was a professor who wrote dozens of business books, my kids are writers. Writing's literally in my DNA.

What's more, I was a practiced writer. I wrote every day, making my living as a commercial writer and journalist. This level of writing is similar to a pianist practicing scales—when the real music comes, they've already got all the skills under their belt.

In other words, when the channeled writing arrived, it was effortless—I knew how to spell, I could type one hundred words a minute, I knew that old rule about "i before e," and so forth. I didn't have to learn anything about writing. What was new is that it was channeling, hearing a voice that wasn't mine, but I got over that pretty fast.

For a full two years, I could only receive through channeled writing. Like many who access their psychic ability later in life, I could only do one thing at first. Then, right around the two-year mark, my voice, and by this I mean my singing voice, began to open. Talk about being surprised! For someone who in all four years of childhood piano lessons had shown absolutely zero musical talent, this was as miraculous as Moses parting the Red Sea.

It was as simple as this: One day I couldn't sing—the next, I could. I was standing in the kitchen, and I opened my mouth to sing a silly song to one of my kids, and this *voice* came out. "What was that?" I remember thinking. And then I sang something else—and the voice stayed. It was almost as if another (very much better!) voice started singing through me. It's not just that my voice got better; it's more as if another voice entered and allowed me to channel it.

Now, I may not sing at the level of a New York opera diva, and I can't read music very well, and my voice certainly can't shatter a wine glass with its soaring high notes, but at the time of this writing, I'm the lead vocalist on three CDs. Two years ago, if someone had told me I'd sing on a CD, I would have fallen off the sofa laughing.

And yet . . .

*We all have wonderful gifts that are waiting to be opened.* We all have the ability to be a channel, a voice, a conduit for the Divine, each in our own unique way.

This can happen instantly, if we surrender and allow ourselves to be utilized.

## Opening Comes When You Are Ready

Let's recap. By the two-year mark, two channeling skills had opened for me:

1. Clairaudience through channeled writing, and
2. Channeling a voice that could sing. (There isn't a term for this. Maybe we should call it *clairsingience!*)

Yet, my other psychic abilities didn't open until I began to receive The 33 Lessons.

Around that same time, a few other channeling tools arrived: some talent for medical intuition, very strong abilities in distance projection, emerging skills in healing and distance healing, and vocalized channeling of other entities' voices. These gifts are still opening.

I now understand that each of my channeling skills has come to me at the exact perfect time—when I'm ready to surrender fully to receive them, and when they will serve the Highest Good. It goes without saying that this will also be your experience—you will receive each new gift at the exactly correct time.

However, many methods of channeling still elude me. For example, I've never seen anyone else's spirit guides. A lot of psychics can do this, but I can't (at least not yet). I've never seen any departed souls with the exception of my father, whom I saw a few times in the months shortly after he died, and both of my grandmothers.

My friend Gregory Kompes, an author and speaker, also found his psychic abilities arriving unexpectedly—and fast. One day he wasn't psychic and the next, he heard from spirit guides, saw departed souls, and had the ability to read people clearly, the whole kit-and-kaboodle!

How will channeling progress for you?

I can only tell you this: your experience will be different from anyone else's.

Remember, you are connecting with the Divine. The Divine understands more than any of us what your purpose is in this life, what soul lessons you need to learn, and how marvelously, beautifully unique you are.

You may receive in only one manner for a long time, and then one day, you might suddenly receive in a new way.

Or, you might simply open like a flower and have instant access to numerous types of receiving all at once, just as a rosebud suddenly blooms under the summer sun.

# 10

## The Six Steps to Channeling

You've already done this process when you did the channeling warm-up. The instructions are the same, but here, I've provided them in a condensed version so you can mark this chapter and use it as your "cheat sheet" every time you channel.

Of course, once you've channeled regularly for a while, you won't need the instructions. You'll be able to go into trance effortlessly and will begin to receive messages, sounds, images, and other experiences.

Here, the six steps to channeling:

1. **Create space.** Find an uninterrupted space of time—an hour is best, but even fifteen minutes will do if that's what you have. Settle yourself in an uninterrupted physical space such as your bedroom, the living room if no one is home, or an empty room you can devote to meditation. Even a quiet corner at work, a park bench, or sitting in your car will work. The key is that you feel safe, have privacy, and won't be distracted by sound or activity. Turn off all the electronica. Ambient music is okay as long as it doesn't distract you (if you need help finding appropriate music, visit www.sarawiseman.com for Mp3 downloads).

2. **Get comfortable.** Sit in the lotus position, if that's comfortable. Otherwise, sit in a comfy chair, with your feet on the floor. Some people like to lie on the ground.

3. **Go into trance.** Close your eyes, take a deep breath in through your nose, let your belly fill up with air, and breathe out through your nose. Repeat this twenty, thirty, fifty, one hundred times. After a time, you will begin to enter a state of trance. The way I experience the transition to trance is as a sudden swoon in my mind—I sense that I'm *going in*, or *going under*. You'll know when it happens.

4. **Adjust your level of trance.** It is effortless to adjust your level of trance. Simply tell yourself, "I'd like to deepen my trance," or "I'd like to lighten my trance," and watch as this happens.

5. **Ask to receive.** Once you're in trance, simply say, "I'm ready to become a channel for Divine guidance today. I'm ready to receive any messages for the Highest Good. Please, tell me what I need to know." If you have a specific question or need help with something, ask for guidance on this issue. Take note of anything you see, hear, or receive. If you are curious about something you notice, ask to see or hear more of it. You may hear voices, see images, or experience something different.

6. **Close the channel.** After at least ten minutes in trance, whether or not you have heard anything or seen anything, say "thank you" to the Divine, and then say aloud or to yourself, "I am closing the channel." When you are ready, come back to the world and open your eyes.

*Note:* If, after a few tries of channeling, it's still difficult to relax your mind, you may find it helpful to use a guided audio recording. You can find these, for both channeling and channeled writing, at www.sarawiseman.com. Now, you don't need to use these, and if you do use them, you won't need them for very long. But especially for people who are very auditory, it can be helpful to have a little "walk through" at the beginning, or for times when you find it difficult to concentrate.

## How Often Should You Channel?

There's no limit to how often you should channel—however, there's probably a limit to how often you'll want to channel! That's because at first you may find the process exhausting; it takes a lot of concentration and uses parts of your brain that you don't normally use.

I'd suggest you go slowly in the beginning, and pace yourself. When I first started, I channeled every day, sometimes several times a day. After long or intense sessions, I'd need a nap. Now, I actively channel at a light level many times a day, and normally don't do deep channeling more than once or twice a week.

The biggest difference? I don't "close" my channel very often, unless I'm in a big crowd or other place where I don't feel like receiving. My window is always purposefully left open, in case my spirit guides have something to say to me or show me.

## How Channeling Will Change Your Life

When I first decided to accept the task of channeling The 33 Lessons, I understood that I was going to be used as a conduit—I was going to let myself step out of the picture, and let something else step in. While it sounds like a no-brainer, it was actually a very hard decision, and a scary one. It's lot easier to tell your kids that you're a novelist than a channel! It's certainly something that I didn't discuss with coworkers and acquaintances:

"Nice to meet you."

"Nice to meet *you*."

"So, what do you do?"

"Oh, mostly sit around receiving messages from spirit guides."

You can see how this might not fly.

But once I started, I never looked back.

Well, that's not true. The truth would be: once I started, I struggled with it for a long time. And finally, I accepted my path, my purpose in this life. And *then* I never looked back.

For reasons unbeknownst to me, being a writer and a channel and receiving channeled writing is what I'm here for in this life—it's what I'm supposed to bring to the world.

Since I began living my life this way—as a channel, a voice, a conduit, in complete surrender to the Divine—my life has changed beyond recognition. Dreams and goals I've had my whole life are now coming into being right before my eyes, without strain.

## Walk Your Own Path

However . . . *not everyone who learns how to channel should make channeling his or her life's work.*

People get confused about this, because when you first learn to channel, it's really exciting, it's really a rush—you walk around in a daze, about as pleased with your new ability as kid who's just learned to ride a two-wheel bicycle (look Ma, no training wheels!). It's very tempting, during this initial discovery of "I can do that?" to start marching around thinking that you need to drop everything in your life and hang out your psychic shingle:

"I'll quit my job!"

"I'll do readings!"

"I'll get a call-in TV show!"

You get the point.

Now, for some of you, this indeed will happen, and for you I say: these steps are going to fall into place so quickly and with such ease, you don't even have to sweat the details.

But for most people, channeling isn't going to be (and isn't meant to be) a replacement for your existing life. Channeling's a tool, and you use it like any other tool you come across—you use a hammer when you need to pound in a nail, and when you don't need to pound nails, you put your hammer safely in your toolbag for later.

For me, I'm a channel—but I'm also a writer, mom, partner, friend, teacher, and singer—and not always in that order. Just because I am a channel does not mean I leave my family and move to Machu Picchu to spend all my waking hours channeling the ancient Divine! No, I am still quite definitely here, making mac and cheese for dinner and doing more laundry than should be permitted by law.

Even though I'm a channel, I'm also supposed to walk my path— and right now, my path includes elbow macaroni.

I also like to kayak, ride my bike, and listen to music way too loudly—not what you'd expect from a channel.

In other words, if you're a dedicated teacher who loves teaching (and who's just learned how to channel), please don't leave your third graders in a lurch in pursuit of the perfect crystal ball. Likewise, if you're a great financial planner who does a great service by helping the checkbook-challenged, please don't quit your job to do readings on late-night radio.

We are all here to walk different paths. Channel, teacher, financial planner—no path is better than another.

If you're doing what you're meant to do here on this earth, there's no better use of your time, energy, and talent. If you're walking toward your destiny, then by all means, use channeling as a tool help you stay on your life's path, the same way you'd use prayer, meditation, being in nature, creative work, service projects, and so on.

But don't abandon your life's work to become a psychic, medium, or channel unless this is in fact your highest calling.

Finally, if all this talk of your life's path has you pretty certain you don't, in fact, know what your life's path is, take a deep breath . . . and relax. Channeling, amazing tool that it is, will help you find out. Simply by tuning into the Divine and asking for clarification and help, you will begin to receive the guidance you need.

II

⟶

# What to Expect When You're Doing Channeled Writing

Channeled writing is a specific technique of channeling that comes most easily to . . . writers.

If you love to write and write frequently in your daily life, either in your work or as your personal passion, if you write stories or articles or in your journal, if you jot things down and make notes, if you read a lot, if you hang out in bookstores and libraries and actually have an opinionated response to the questions "Do you have a favorite pen?" and "Do you prefer college rule or narrow?" it's likely that you're going to be quite suited to channeled writing.

For me, channeling through writing was an easy, natural progression because I make my living as a writer—I literally spend hours writing each day. I mean, think of it from the Divine's point of view:

*Wanted: Scribe to take down Divine guidance for 33 total Lessons. Must have good writing skills, be able to spell, type quickly, and be willing to sit in a chair and write six hours a day without complaint.*

Yep, that just about sums up my writing skills. I have the talent to string words together, one after the other, *ad infinitum.* Most days I have the patience to sit in the chair, which as any productive writer will tell you is the only reason any writing gets done at all. I type so fast that I actually have no letters left on half of my computer keys—they've been rubbed off by the ferocity of my typing! I have the tenacity to go through page upon page of manuscript, correcting, editing, and so forth. (In fact, I just made a correction right here!) I have the knowledge of how to proofread for typos, which even the Divine requires.

If you are a strong writer, if you love words and writing, chances are good that you're going to be a strong channeled writer. You don't have to be as strong a writer, but it helps. The process isn't difficult—all it takes is knowing how.

## Examples from The Truths

When you read The 33 Lessons later in this book, you'll notice that it has a certain writing style—a clear voice, organized in a specific Lesson. For example, take a look at this language:

> Your life's path, your life's purpose, is what is required by your perfect soul, for your perfect soul's growth. It is measured by your earth heart's growth.
>
> The ability to see beauty, to have compassion, to know what it is to give and to receive love, to enlarge your heart so much that it contains room for all of humanity, and then to ask to receive more—to make room for all of the Holy Ones, for room to place yet another Jesus in your heart, yet another Mohammed, yet another saint or ascended master, and then to add in all the other Holy Ones in the universe, even who you do not know of yet, but who some of you will know in time. To continue to add in everyone—friend, family, enemy, into your heart, until your heart is filled to bursting.
>
> And then to add another.
>
> And to do all of this without fear, my friend. Without fear. To continually open your heart.
>
> For the earth heart bends and breaks, and the earth heart can be wounded, but in each measure of this exists the inten-

tion and possibility of it becoming larger, to enlarge itself until it is the size of the universe, which as you know is unlimited and unending.

Thus, your life's purpose is this. Your life's path is this. To expand your heart until it is the size of the universe. Any other measure of your life's path—as to what is your calling, what should you do—this is deeply given to you, for you are unique in your talents and your abilities that you may give to the world.

You may affect many, you may affect a few. The number is not what is important.

But you must walk in the world with your earth heart ever compassionate and ever expanding, growing bigger with each day, growing bigger always, and you must do this without fear.

This is the purpose of your life.

That's beautiful! I love it! When I received this, it made me cry—I sat and received and wept and wrote, and felt my heart open yet again. But not all channeled writing sounds this way; in fact, what different people receive (or even what one person receives at different times, or from different guides) can be enormously diverse.

For example, here's one of The Truths I received from Hajam earlier. The tone, the topic, the wording—it's quite different from The 33 Lessons:

Death does not change much.
Death is as simple as sliding behind the veil.
The veil is pale yellow or golden, shimmering with light. Some say it looks like a shower curtain, and I am afraid to report that they are right.
You can pull the veil open or closed at will. The people who pass through, who come to this place beyond the veil . . . they may or may not stay there for long.
It is like a holding pen, a gathering place, a train station, or a giant entrance hall, where you wait, with others, until it is your time to move to the next place.

You do not have to be dead to see it. You can access this other dimension, this separate universe, at any time. At least some of you can.

Those who are more advanced, or who have learned the trick, can casually close their eyes and in a simple, effortless movement flick the filmy, shimmering shower curtain open, a gentle clacking and rolling as it moves . . . well, these same people can also slide back and forth between the worlds: earth world, spirit world, present, future, past, life, death, and what is indubitably beyond death, beyond imagining, all matter, all energy in perfect blissful union.

But even for the others, who do not have the knack . . . sometimes, this can happen too. For the veil is always fluttering. And sometimes, there is a small gap, similar to what you see when you look at the parting of clouds on a bright summer day, and you imagine that you can see God. Sometimes, this happens. When you least expect it, without effort or knowledge, a crack appears, as if someone has left the curtain open for just a second, and you can see into the next dimension.

It is at this moment that glimpses of other worlds, our ancestors, the people we love who have passed on, the future, the infinite, the eternal Now, become possible. Even for those who are not paying attention. Even those who refuse to look.

Sometimes, you can see them just behind the veil—everyone you ever loved who has died, waiting there in the great gathering hall, milling around and talking to each other, and they might greet you too, their faces will light up as you see them, and they can see you.

You can pull the curtain open—try it now.

Breathe in. Breathe out. Look at the hum of particles hanging in the air. We are all this, this hum and drone. The smallest things shift and move, they fizz and gather. It is the same everywhere. It is all like this.

Look with new eyes.

⊷◈⊶

# Examples from Other Writers

Another collection of channeled writings described as "communication from God" recently came to light with the work of the late Phillip Allen Moss. His *The Second Book of Proverbs*, a collection of scribbled scraps of paper, was given to his son, poet Richard Wilson Moss in 1973, with the instructions to publish it. According to his daughter-in-law, the author was memorialized by the priests at Loyola College in Baltimore as walking in Jesus Christ's footsteps and often taught classes there with no education himself because the priests found him enlightening. Many publishers' rejections later, his work was self-published by his son. When I first came across this work, I was stunned by its wisdom. It is both sacred and profane, and that it is Divine, I am certain—there is a truth to these writings that send chills down my spine.

Here, an excerpt from Phillip Allen Moss:

1. philosophers write philosophy
2. garbage men write garbage
3. do not search for your identity
4. it is not that you have no identity
5. it is that there is no identity
6. in all eternity there is no identity
7. you can describe
8. you cannot identify
9. a child shall not lead us
10. there are no children
11. those who know where they are going don't
12. those who are content aren't
13. to be afraid of the unknown is to be infinitely afraid
14. to be fearless is stupid
15. the balance of fear necessary for perpetuation is unreal
16. to be able to see the immensity of existence would be to dissolve in a cataclysm of awesomeness
17. our vision of existence is unreal

18. if your eyes were opened you would be destroyed with awareness
19. we strive to understand
20. there is no such thing as understanding
21. to gaze at a flower is all there is
22. a turtle on a log in the sun is all there is
23. there is only the mindless mind of man
24. there are no turtles or logs or suns
25. existence is only in the mind of man
26. do not seek
27. there is nothing to find
28. a fish cannot be wet
29. a person cannot understand

Another man I know, Gary Weber, has practiced channeled writing his entire adult life. As the universe would have it, I met him shortly after I began receiving The Truths—he lived two blocks from my house.

I'd met his son a few weeks earlier, and for some reason had mentioned that I was doing channeled writing. I don't know why—I hadn't told anyone else. Immediately he said, "My dad does that," and I met Gary a week or so later. But it wasn't until four years later, after I'd received The 33 Lessons, that Gary and I sat down to compare notes.

Gary has practiced channeled writing for more than fifty years, following in his mother's footsteps.

"When I was a boy, I used to sit with my hand on top of hers, and feel the energy flowing through it," he told me. Gary dreamt and wrote about 9/11 before it happened, and his writing always takes deep notice of acts of terrorism and disaster. He writes by hand, and always uses a pencil (we all have our preferences). A psychologist for many years with the State of Oregon, he has channeled thousands of pages.

As we talked, I was struck by the similarity of how we received, and the content of much of our writing. Here, a sample of what Gary Weber received:

> Right living is purposeful, engaged and directed to the ascension of spiritual growth. That is not to mean "holy", to be moral does not mean to be holy. Living and dying are connected as your soul does not cease when you die. In a manner of speaking, it awakes, and is changed for better or worse by the previous incarnation. What seems to be a very long process of living is considered to be a fragment by the spirit upon physical death.

And another:

> Some have asked whether God is a separate Entity from man, or whether man is a part of God, or whether part of man is a part of God.
>
> We say God and man are one. They are not separate entities. Man is a co-creator with God, because man is also God; you cannot separate the two. When man acts in ungodly ways it is the error or denying his godliness, and that is why it is twice tragic. Tragic for the act of barbarism itself, and also tragic for the denial of the Godness of the person.

Terri Daniel, author of *A Swan In Heaven: Conversations Between Two Worlds*, is another receiver of amazing channeled writings. These come to her through the voice of her late son, Danny Mandell, who lost his ability to speak during the last few years of a degenerative childhood illness. He died as a teen, and from the moment of his death, Terri has been able to channel truly extraordinary messages from him. Here, an excerpt from what Terri received from him:

> To solve problems in human life, there is no other guidance and no other source of information than the Higher Self, which receives its messages directly from God, and God is an energy that

burns and energizes us like a pilot light. If you want to receive the truth, ask from the Higher Self, not from the ego. For example, the ego asks, "Should I stay in this marriage or should I leave?" But the Higher Self asks, "Lead me to whatever best serves the truth and allows me to live according to my core value and to do what I came here on earth to do."

And another:

All the truths, the secrets if you will, are always available to those living on earth, and these truths never change. Different beings on earth tap into them and express them at different times in different ways, but there can't be anything new because they're universal truths.

⊸◇⊸

## What Will You Receive?

Of course, what you receive might not sound like any of these—in fact, I'm sure it won't. Why? As a unique individual, you will channel in your own way, with your own style and language.

In other words, yes, you are a channel, but you're definitely not generic!

All channeled writing is different—it sounds different, covers different information, and will have different uses of language. Some of you will receive information that is quite familiar to you, in your specific interest area. For example, if you've always been interested in Mary, you may discover that you easily channel messages from Mary, or information about her works.

If you have strong personality traits, expect those traits to come through—extroverts will have no problem talking to their spirit guides and pestering them with questions, whereas introverts may hunker down and stick to the task of listening, working hard to catch the nuances of what their guides say.

If you are a flowery writer, your channeled writing may be more lyrical or poetic. If you're a straightforward writer, your channeled writing may be direct and uncomplicated, and so on.

However, this also depends on the idiosyncrasies of your guide. Hajam's Truths have a poetic tone—some of it's almost literary. With my guides for The 33 Lessons, there are also differences: with Constance, there's a dryness or reserve to her delivery. Miriam is convoluted and difficult to follow. Gabriel was the most soothing—I almost forgot to write down what he said, I was so happy to be in his presence.

Your guides will sound different from each other, too.

Some guides have normal-sounding, modern voices in your native language. Some have accents or dialects. Some have what I can only call "angelic" voices—ancient, unfamiliar voices with odd inflections and archaic wordings. Or, you might hear the familiar voice of your grandmother, her soft, Midwestern twang.

Some guides speak fast, some drawl. Some have lot to say and will provide you with teachings that are meant for a larger audience than just yourself. Others offer sweet words of encouragement that are meant for you only—messages that are a source of enormous personal comfort to you.

I don't know exactly what your channeled writings will be like.

But I do know they will be uniquely, completely yours.

## Channeled Writing Is Personal

The sample writings by Phillip Allen Moss, Gary Weber, and what I received in The 33 Lessons and The Truths are more global. They are teachings, meant for a broad audience. But when I first started channeled writing, I used it almost exclusively to help me figure out my own stuff. I was in a state of great confusion, a dark night of the soul, some might say. I'd created a lot of upheaval for my kids in getting divorced, quitting my job for no very good reason, and turning my attention to writing.

I didn't know why I had to do these things, I just knew that I had to do them.

What I found out is that once you make the leap, the safety net does appear—but sometimes it sure seems like an invisible net! There you are, out on the tightrope, and you're pretty sure the net's there, but . . . what if it isn't? I mean, everyone says, "The net will appear" but why can't you see it? What if instead of being guided by the Divine, you are actually making the worst mistake of your life? Heading into free fall?

Well, you're not.

But I didn't know that then. As I walked the tightrope, hoping and praying there was a net beneath me, my personal channeled writing (mostly questions to my spirit guides), gave me infinite comfort and sustenance. Here, some examples:

This answer, in response to whether I should move myself and my children to a new home with my new partner.

> Gather your things. And make your home. Turn out the old, tear it up and move it. Bring down the castles, bring down the barrels. Bring up the hard things and move them all in. The answers are coming to you as in your dream. The answers continue. There will be money, you do not need to worry. We want you to write, and to think, and to be still and alone with your thoughts. We are giving you the time, and the space to do this.

This answer, in response for a plea for guidance at a time when I had received still more rejections on my writing and did not have a steady paycheck; I wondered if I should get a regular job again.

> Keep going. We do not say this because it is ample, ambient sound, we say this because this is what you can do, you can keep going, and this is what will refine you, this is what will refinish you. We understand that seems hopeless at this point, so close

and yet so far, so impossible. But we say to you, this will be what happens.

Do not worry. It is normal to be tired and exhausted, you are healing even still, even though you believe you have already healed, it is not true; you have much still to heal yourself with.

We are here in the room with you, even as you do the normal things.

All things do not have to be successful. It seems hopeless, how you have been working for others, so much and for so long, and how no one seems to be working for you. But this is not the case. We are even now arranging things so that they will be in the right way for you.

The question, and the answer. This next is especially interesting for me to read now, as this was answered nearly two years before I received The 33 Lessons, or even knew that I would receive them.

*Please help me to know what to do with my career. Not even my career, but what I am to say; what I am to bring to the world with my voice.*

You are to bring the word that we are giving you. You do not need to worry about what to say, because we will tell you. The ideas that we will bring you are spiritual in nature, they involve the needs of society, they involve what people need to know. It may not be your voice; it may be ours. You do not need to be afraid. Doors will open with each thing that you present to higher editors, and with each you will build doors to open higher still.

You have what you need, your writing is good enough; you do not need to learn more. You already know what to do; we are here. We are here to move you along faster, to get you to where you must go faster. There is a sense of little time, but this is not true.

People do not die as you believe. They do stay in a different place.

The Divine will direct even the angels. They too know serendipity; they know it all. You don't know how? Let us write it for you. You don't know how? You do not need to know anything.

If I had not received this channeled writing at this time, this affirmation from the universe, I would have quit writing. I would not have had the courage to move myself and my children into a new home. I would never, never have been able to say yes when The 33 Lessons came.

Fortunately, and even in the midst of all my mistakes and confusion and personality flaws, my spirit guides kept me on track.

## Channeled Writing Gives Clear Guidance

If you're a strong writer, or a person who works easily with language and words, you will find that channeled writing gives you more clear direction than simple channeling.

Remember, when you channel you either receive a) clairvoyantly, which is symbolic, or b) clairaudiently, via a voice you hear. You'll receive in pictures or words, in your mind's eye, or in your mind's ear.

However, when you write things down in channeled writing, you receive messages in writing that you can read later. This means there is less chance of misinterpreting or forgetting the message.

For example, let's say that during an intuitive reading for someone, I channel the following clairvoyantly, through my psychic seeing:

*I see a house with an open door and there's a woman inside beckoning to you. The woman has a large blue hat, and she says she's your mother. She's holding a large fish out to you, as a gift. Your new boyfriend is there, and as she walks by him, she sniffs loudly in the air. This is significant.*

That's what I see, and that's what I state to my client during the reading. Certainly, there's more analysis to be done to understand this message.

However, if you receive this information using channeled writing, the message might be written down like this:

*Your mother is concerned for you. She asks you to come to her table, eat a family meal. She thinks there's something fishy about your new boyfriend—she wonders if you can smell it too.*

As I recommended before, if you are emotionally delicate right now, in a very difficult phase in your life, or have trouble separating yourself from the voice you receive while doing channeled writing, I'd suggest you take a break and use the tools of prayer or meditation instead. You will still enjoy a direct connection with the Divine, but it will be at a gentler pace that will be easier for you to handle.

## A Style of Writing that Is Not Your Own

You may receive a style and use of language that is not how you normally write. When I received The Truths, they dealt with subjects I didn't know about, and had a rhythm and cadence that wasn't mine. The 33 Lessons were almost archaic in their language structure—they used ways of composing sentences that I'd never allow in my own writing. This was an old-fashioned, plainspoken kind of language, with wording from a few centuries ago. It definitely wasn't modern. All four of the entities I have received from so far (Hajam, Constance, Miriam, and Gabriel) showed up as unique voices and appeared differently on the page.

**The use of "we" or "you" rather than "I."** My experience is that spiritual entities, one or more, will always speak in the collective "we." I believe this is because, as ascended beings, they understand what it is to be a part of the collective hum—the universal, cosmic energy that is Now. Spirit guides and angels will speak directly to you, or with a name of endearment, such as "beloved," "daughter," "child," "darling," or your most silly nickname ever. They will call you what you long to be called. They love you. They will speak to you in a way that touches your heart.

**Fanciful or foreign language.** I am always amazed at the word choices used by spirit guides. This is why it is *so* important to listen carefully. Imagine you're listening to someone via a shaky cell phone line—there might be static, it's hard to hear. Even without static, you may not understand what you're hearing. I couldn't understand

Hajam's name until after three weeks of guessing, when I finally asked him to spell it. Before that, I kept hearing (no joke, this is what I thought it was) "Hava Nagila"!

You may also receive words in other languages—and this can be very confusing! For one thing, if you don't know how to speak the language you are receiving, you won't know how to spell the words. Do your best. Ask your guides to speak slowly. Ask them to spell out words for you.

While I've read of ancient saints and mystics who received messages and wrote flawlessly in other languages they did not know, I have not seen or experienced this yet.

## Write It Down, Exactly

Write down what you hear, even if you don't like it. Sometimes you may have an emotional response to what you're hearing and get scared, or you'll hear something you don't want to hear, and this will make it harder for you to receive.

You know how when someone tells you something you don't want to hear (but that you know is true) and you hold your hands over your ears and say "la, la, la" like a little kid? The same thing happens in channeled writing, when you hear what you don't want hear (but you know is true).

La, la, la!

Take your hands off your ears, grit your teeth, and *write it down.* Use exact words, as precisely as you can. If you're not sure, say something like this:

"What is this word?"

"Can you spell this word?"

"I still can't hear you."

If you still can't tell what a word is, just leave a blank and keep writing.

Why is it important to write down exactly what you hear, even if it doesn't make sense to you? For one thing, it may make sense later. You may be receiving information about future events that you can't begin to fathom. So even if you don't understand it, just write it down. For example, when I was doing some channeled writing about meeting my partner (who wasn't even a glimmer in my eye yet), I wrote this:

*You will meet a spiritual man. You will meet him in a coffee shop, or a music lobby.*

I wrote this reluctantly, thinking, "Oh, silly me, there I go again, not listening carefully, writing nonsense."

Yet, six months later, I did meet this man. We'd both signed up for a class held at a coffee shop, and officially, the first day of class was our first meeting. However, the day we *really* met was a few months later, when we both, separately and unbeknownst to the other, attended a Prince concert in the city. Along with the thirty thousand other people in attendance, I was cruising through the main lobby before the show, when I suddenly crashed into a stranger—I literally fell into his arms.

Mortified, I muttered, "Excuse me," and tried to extricate myself.

But this guy wasn't letting go! Struggling to get away, I looked up and saw my classmate's beaming face, smiling at me.

"Oh, it's you!" I exclaimed in recognition, and then, as the flash suddenly hit me of who this man was going to be in my life, I repeated, "Oh, it's you!" Our relationship began in that instant.

A coffee house? A music lobby? Flipping through the pages of my past-channeled writing, I saw the words written there in black and white, and had to laugh. Yep, those guides sure had one over on me! There it was, just like they'd said six months earlier, when I had no idea what I was writing, or what it would mean. I was glad I'd written it down, because I'd have never believed it.

This is so important that I need to say it again: write down exactly what you hear, even if you don't know what it means. If your guides tell you that you will live on a farm in Wisconsin and raise Shetland ponies, even though you currently live in a city apartment and have never set foot in a barn, just write it down.

Then see what happens.

## Common Experiences

### CLARIFICATION THAT YOU NEED TO CHANGE YOUR PATH

Sometimes, Divine guidance will be gentle—yet persistent. You will begin to receive the same messages over and over. For example, "You should take up karate," or "Take your car to the mechanic," or "Your marriage is in danger," or "Your stomach is not healthy."

After receiving the same messages a few times, you'll hopefully realize that this information is being given to you as a gift—a reminder, a suggestion, something that would be good for you to follow sooner rather than later. If you receive the message that something is wrong with your stomach, I would not hesitate to make an appointment with your physician or health practitioner. If you hear a suggestion that you should go back to school, for example, you might want to start looking at some schools to attend. Your movement in that direction will give your guides the energy boost they need to set things in motion.

### A Funny Thing About Divine Guidance?

Sometimes it's not very direct. For example, say you receive the message "go back to school," and you follow up by researching schools. You do some preliminary research online, but then you decide to visit some schools in person. Sure enough, when you walk into the admissions office of the school you're visiting, boom, there he or she is—the person of your dreams. Or, as you're driving to visit this school, boom, there it is—a highly desirable property, the kind of thing you've always wanted, at a great price, and the owner wants to sell it to you.

That sort of thing.

Sometimes the Divine takes you from Point A to Point B. But just as often, the Divine takes you from Point A to Point B . . . to Point C, D, E, F—before you finally get to G. (And of course after you get to G, you will most certainly be moving on to H, I, J and so forth! There is no end to your life's journey.)

You never know where Divine guidance will lead you. But each time you follow the guidance you receive, even if you don't understand why, you'll be led to the next step on your path. Even if you don't know where you're going, the Divine does. As long as you listen and follow, the Divine will take you to the next place you are supposed to be.

## Delayed Reactions

When you channel writing or information that you don't want to hear, you may not have a reaction until later. You might be aware of grief, or anger, or a variety of emotions—you might even have tears streaming down your face as you write, but you can be trying so hard to concentrate on receiving that you hold the emotion at arm's length. "Gotta stay focused. I'll get to that later," you mumble, as you try to get the writing down.

It isn't until after you've finished the channeled writing, when you're in the midst of eating a veggie on rye, that the emotions begin to arrive.

At this point, half a sandwich in hand, tears dripping down your cheeks, you may even be tempted to say things like

- "This channeled writing stuff isn't for real," or
- "It's just stuff my mind made up," or
- "I must have gotten some bad spirits."

Well, tell yourself what you want. The emotions you feel are genuine. When you look at what you have written, in three months, in six months, in a year, everything will be set out clearly—you'll see that what you wrote was not only accurate, but beyond what you are able to imagine now.

For example, let's say you are headed for divorce, but you don't know this yet. You still think you can save your marriage. And yet, in your channeled writing today, you write that you will leave your husband and move to another state within three years. You're sobbing as you write this, because you know in your heart that this is true. Even though you don't want to get divorced and you have no plans to abandon the marriage.

Your logical mind, the one that's angrily wiping the tears away, says, "There's no way this writing can be true!"

It's shocking. It's horrifying. This information arrives out of the blue (or so it seems).

Your heart knows it's true, but this information is not welcome to you. If you have a certain kind of personality, you may be tempted to throw your laptop or notebook across the floor. If you have another kind of personality, you'll feel an enormous sadness in your heart.

Disbelief. Anger. Sadness. Rebellion. Grief. Fear. Doubt. Rage. Anxiety. And so on. You'll feel them all in channeled writing.

Channeled writing brings you Divine guidance. This includes information you want to hear—as well as information you don't want to hear.

## INFORMATION YOU NEED NOW

Not all channeled writing foretells the future. Much of it deals with immediate emotional issues that face you right now, right this moment. Your guides might write, "You have been worried," or "You feel sad." And this clear, loving statement from your spirit guides or angels will be enough for you to reach for the tissues.

Your guides are entities of pure love and compassion. They are here to help you. You may be crazy with sadness, relief, guilt, grief, anger, confusion—whatever feelings you are carrying, they will take this burden from you. The pain of your emotion gets carried away on their shoulders, not yours, and you will feel a sense of great peace.

## TIME AND SPACE DISSOLVING

Going into trance allows you to experience time and space in a new way. When you sit in trance, whether you are channeling or doing channeled writing, you may lose track of time. You may receive for an hour, two hours, without feeling much of anything—no boredom, no need to shift your position, no need to eat or drink anything or go to the bathroom—you're completely connected into the bliss of direct connection with the Divine. You understand that time and space are malleable, nonlinear, all connected, all constant, all One.

This is awesome—but it can wreak havoc on your schedule!

I had a lot of problems with this at the beginning of my channeling practice, thinking I'd go into trance for fifteen minutes, and two hours later I'd come out, realizing that my kids were waiting on the front steps of the school. In fact, this has happened so often that now I give myself a time before I enter trance, as in, "I will be finished with this session by 2:45 p.m., so I won't be late for the kids." When I do this, I automatically come out of trance at the moment I requested. (Try this yourself—you'll be amazed at how easy it is.)

A note of caution: Many people use candles, incense, smudge sticks, and other things that burn to heighten the trance experience. Please, be careful. When you are in trance, you simply won't be able to attend to burning flames, pots on the stove, babies who need to be watched, and so forth.

## A HEADACHE

Especially if you're new to meditating and prayer, but even if you're not, expect to have a little headache when you journey into trance. Does this go away with time? It depends on what else you have going on in your life. Sometimes I nap after channeled writing, sometimes

I jump into the full beat of my day. Sometimes the headache goes away, sometimes it lingers. Each time is different.

If you do get a headache, drink a glass of water, take a shower, soak in a hot bath, take a nap, eat something, go watch a few minutes of a funny DVD, check your email. In other words, come back to your earth reality. Chances are good your headache will go away soon.

If you feel really tired after your channeled writing session, remind yourself that you probably aren't really tired—you're probably overwhelmed. This is fine! You've just processed a lot of emotions and healing. Soul growth is hard work, and feeling different is to be expected. Rest, take the day off—whatever you require.

## Awe and Bliss

You may feel overwhelmed by the beauty and love of your spirit guides and angels. You may experience a sense of awe when you are in the presence of Holy Ones. While we are human, they are exalted beings who radiate an ineffable goodness and love. It is simply grand to be with them—they bring peace and comfort to the heart.

If you haven't meditated or prayed before, you may also feel something very exciting the first time you do channeled writing—you may experience ecstatic bliss. It's wonderful! Enjoy it! The more you go into trance and have a direct connection with the Divine, whether for channeling or channeled writing, meditation or prayer, the better you're going to feel.

# 13

## Channeled Writing: The Practice

### Ground Rules for Channeled Writing

First, let's put it in perspective: when you receive channeled writing, you're connecting with the Divine.

This is the real thing, and it's beyond powerful.

Thus, the most important ground rule you can set in channeled writing is that you'll use it only to receive Divine guidance *for the Highest Good.*

Not just for your Highest Good either . . . but also for your neighbor's Highest Good . . . and even your enemy's Highest Good.

Interested in getting weird, half-baked entities to come forward and do parlor tricks for you? You can do that. But do it elsewhere, please, and don't use this book. In true channeling of the Divine, there is no room for trappings and trickery.

Seriously. An angel, a Holy Being, is going to come in and sit by your shoulder and tell you magnificent things to write.

Why mess with that?

# Practice for Laptop or Computer

If you are a decent typist, a laptop is far and away the best method to use for channeled writing. Computers also work well, but they limit you to sitting at a desk. I find it most comfortable to sit on a sofa with my laptop, so that I can comfortably go into trance. I often have a blanket over my legs or shoulders, as I tend to get extremely cold when I'm channeling.

If you're not a good typist or want to do channeled writing with pen and paper, we'll cover that in the next section.

How to know which method—laptop or handwritten—will work best for you? Answer these questions:

1. Do you type easily?

2. Do you type quickly?

3. Have you been trained in typing or keying?

4. Can you take dictation as quickly as someone speaks, even if you make a lot of typos?

5. Can you type without looking at the keyboard? (Hunt-and-peckers should answer no.)

6. Can you type with eyes closed? (Before you say no, try it.)

If you answered yes to most of these questions, you're a good candidate for using a laptop or computer. However, if you struggle with typing, you're better off using pen and paper.

Now, the Divine does not care which technique you use! You could use stone tablets if you wanted (Moses did). Your guides want you to be comfortable, and to work without fear or frustration. Just plain old channeling is a brand-new skill for most of you, and now you're ratcheting up the learning curve even more. That means, whatever method sounds easier (laptop, computer, by hand, in crayon) is the one that's right for you.

Feeling nervous? Not sure if it's going to work?

It will.

## CREATING SPACE

Just as when you channel, you'll need a quiet, private space. Again, I like working sitting on a sofa or cozy chair. Sometimes I work sitting up in bed.

Make sure you have plenty of battery power, at least an hour, or plug into an outlet. Next, create a file, name it, and save it. Doing this part *now* is important—when you're in trance, chances are good that you'll forget to save, or have some problem with saving your file. Before I made this part of my practice, I'd forget to hit save or hit a wrong key with my eyes closed, and poof, suddenly the whole document was gone. (You probably won't have this problem. Heck, maybe you'll have new problems!) If you do have technical difficulties or lose information, don't worry about it too much—because this guidance is Divine, if you received it once, you'll receive it again.

Now, just as you did for channeling, lock the front door, tell the kids to go to the neighbors, turn off the stereo, the TV, your cell phone, and take it easy on the music. Ambient music such as you'd use for yoga, meditation, or to get a massage is fine, but save the rock and roll for later.

Next, rest your fingers lightly on your keyboard, so as to remind your body what you're going to do. As often happens during trance, sometimes your fingers will fall on the wrong keys—and stay there. There you are, blithely typing *akdjfdlsierowsfkjsdfjweoirjwaepaoifj* for twenty minutes.

Oh, well. Sometimes this happens! Don't worry about it. Remember, Divine guidance is constant and eternal. You will always receive what you need to receive.

Also, don't be concerned if your fingers feel cold, stiff, clumsy, or as if they aren't working right. This is common. Similarly, you don't have to curl your fingers a certain way, or hold your wrist at a certain angle, so long as you are comfortable.

There's no right way.

At this point, all you're doing is resting your fingers on the keyboard, lightly and easily, the way a pianist might place her fingers gently on the keys right before she settles in to play.

## Go Into Trance

Now, with your fingers resting in a relaxed state on the keyboard, close your eyes and begin to breathe deeply in through the nose, taking the air into your belly, and breathing out again through the nose.

Breathe this way for ten cycles, then continue on for twenty, thirty, however many you want. Go into a light trance, and hang out there. After a certain point, forget about your breathing—you'll use your breathing to take you into trance, but once you're in, your body goes on automatic and you can forget about concentrating on it.

Once you've found your comfortable level of trance, remind yourself that you're going to channel in words, using your laptop or your computer. You may still see images, and you will definitely hear a voice, but remind yourself that you're going to receive this information as writing. You are going to act as scribe, and you are going to write down what you hear.

Go ahead and tell yourself this now by saying in your mind or aloud, "I'm going to channel through writing."

## Creating Intent

Next, while you are in trance, create intent for what you would like to receive. To do this, simply say something in your mind like, "Dear God, please allow me to receive any messages that you would like me to know." If you have a specific question, ask it now, but I find it's better to be open to what the Divine wants to tell you. For example, if you need guidance about your job situation, you might say, "Dear

God, please allow me to receive any messages that you would like me to know—and by the way, I especially need guidance about my job."

You have now effectively opened the window between you and the Divine, and you may begin to feel a soft, peaceful feeling spreading throughout your body. I have heard this feeling of connection described in many ways—body filled with light, a sense of peace, tranquility, serenity, bliss, love, Oneness.

For me, it's a state of knowing I've made a direct connection—I'm now in communication with the Divine. It's a feeling of bliss but with the most precise attention paid. It is the essence of existing right in the Now, in connection with God. Sometimes I'll feel very cold or notice myself shaking; sometimes I'll forget that I have a body anymore.

But, even though you're blissing out, don't forget you have a job to do!

Remain in trance, set your hands lightly on the keyboard (make sure your fingers are on the right keys!) and type in this message: "Dear God, please allow me to receive any messages that you would like me to know."

Use your own words if you like.

Try to keep your eyes closed during the rest of the process, so that your trance is not interrupted. Breathe in, breathe out, and wait for your channeled writing to arrive.

How long will you need to wait? I don't know. You may feel the urge to write right away—if this happens, begin writing. If nothing comes, wait some more. Time isn't particularly important right now; if nothing arrives immediately, just hang out in trance and enjoy it. There's nothing you can do "right" or "wrong" at this point.

What happens to most people is that they suddenly *know* they need to write a particular word or sentence.

Or, you might hear words form in your mind—at first you might even think it's your own voice, or that you're making stuff up. Perish the thought! The minute you hear a voice—even if it is your own internal voice—please begin writing down what it says. Keep your eyes closed, don't worry about typos, and key in what you hear.

Sometimes, the act of writing from your own voice triggers channeled writing.

And sometimes, what we think is our own voice at first turns out to be a very different voice indeed.

At this point, you're still in a light trance, and you may or may not have written anything. But you'll definitely be feeling like you want to write, you're ready to write, you're itching to get going.

Allow yourself to hear the voices that come to you, whether they sound like your own voice or that of a spirit guide. Ask again, "What would you like me to know?" and key in what comes to you.

You may type a few words. You may type sentences, paragraphs. Some of you will type many pages. I don't know what will happen. But something will.

If you have the sudden urge to write something crazy, something you don't understand (the word *rutabaga*, for example), don't question it. Just write it down. You never know where the Divine is taking you!

Stay in your light trance, and continue typing until the message is complete.

If you're not sure if the message is complete, go ahead and ask your spirit guide or angel or voice in your head, "Is there anything else you'd like me to know?" Now's also a good time to ask some questions if you need clarification: "What else do I need to know about rutabagas?" or "I don't understand what you meant about rutabagas; can you tell me in a different way?"

CLOSING THE CHANNEL

When you've finally received whatever you're going to receive, the connection will become weak. Suddenly you won't hear a clear voice anymore, you'll be straining to hear, and then you won't hear anything. When this happens, say "thank you," and then say, "I am closing the channel" in your mind or aloud. Next, slowly bring yourself out of trance. If you want to stay in trance for a while, this is fine. Just recognize that the channeled writing portion of your trance is complete.

That whole saving-your-work thing? Do it now.

Once you're done, with your work safely saved, you may be tempted to analyze what you've written—but I suggest you don't do that now. Take a quick peek if you must, but that's it. What you've received through channeled writing will already be in your head, no matter how deep a trance you were in; you don't need to revisit it at this time.

Instead, shut down your laptop or computer, and get up and do something else—put in a load of laundry, empty the dishwasher, eat lunch, go out for a walk with the dog, have a cup of tea, meet some friends, go for a run, whatever it is that makes you feel normal and grounded.

The reason for doing relaxed, effortless, everyday kinds of things is that right now, after experiencing a direct connection with the Divine, you may feel a little spacey, a little floaty, a little blissed out, a little overstimulated. It's important to give yourself time to make the transition.

It's not a bad idea to have some private time set aside, as the people you come into contact with directly after doing channeled writing may seem especially jarring or irritating. They're actually not acting any worse than they usually do—the problem is that right now *you're* different. Give yourself some time to adjust as you come out of trance and return to your regular self.

Take note that your "regular" self has changed.

Remember, every time you practice channeling and channeled writing, you will experience soul growth. Every time you connect with the Divine, you will be transformed.

This means that your reality—your life as you know it now—will also begin to change in ways that support this new, more evolved you.

# Practice for Writing by Hand

For those of you who will do channeled writing by hand, we'll need to introduce the idea of *the soft gaze*. This is a technique long used by yogis and mystics, in which you enter into trance with your eyes closed, and then you slightly open your eyes. However, instead of focusing only on what's in front of you, you sense the whole room, seeing what's near, far, in front of you, behind you, above and below you, all at the same time.

Try this now.

Close your eyes and breathe deeply until you feel the beginning of trance coming over you—then open your eyes very slightly.

Do you notice how you can "see" more of the room than you thought? You have an awareness of what's nearby, what's to the left and right, even what's behind you. (Interestingly, this is a technique you might use if you were practicing astral projection, or viewing past and future. However, right now, we're just concentrating on the soft gaze as a tool for channeled writing.)

This soft gaze allows you to look at your journal (in order to keep your writing hand moving properly from left to right without going off the page) while not actively paying attention to the words you are writing.

Why?

Because the fastest way to get channeled writer's block is to read what you're channeling while you're channeling it!

Another reason for using the soft gaze? If you focus too clearly on your notebook, you won't be able to maintain trance. You'll be sitting there worrying about everything that's happening: "What if I don't hear anything to write?" What if I don't understand what I hear?" "I definitely don't understand what I just wrote." "I wrote *that*?"

Stop that!

Go into trance, and stay there. Then open your eyes in soft gaze, and let it happen.

## Use the Soft Gaze

Practice the soft gaze now, while you are looking around the room. Again, sit quietly, eyes closed, and allow yourself to go into a light trance. When you feel a relaxed, blissful state arriving, open your eyes slightly, but let your lids keep on feeling heavy.

How heavy? Well, think of how you feel when you're just waking up in the morning—your alarm clock's ringing, you're reaching for the snooze button, you've turned it off. *Ah . . . more zzzzs.*

This is how your eyes feel now. Heavy, lidded, half-closed, sleepy, hazy—you're here, but not quite here. You're in trance, but still aware. You can see your hand in relation to the page of your journal, but you're not focused on or distracted by the words you're writing.

## Begin the Practice

Now that you've got the soft gaze mastered, you're ready to start. The nice thing about a journal is that you can curl up anywhere, and you don't need any batteries or plug-ins.

You already know how to set your intent for the Highest Good. Now, begin by going into a light trance. Breathe in, breathe out, breathe deep into the belly. Breathe out. Ahhh! A few more repetitions, and you're ready to let the trance arrive. All this time, you've got your journal open, and your pen is lightly in your hand, resting lightly on the page.

The next step is to ask to receive. Say, in your mind or aloud, something along the lines of, "Please let me receive what I should know, in writing." And then put your pen to your paper and let yourself begin to write.

If you've tried channeled writing with a laptop or computer, you'll understand right away that this is a different process. It's more intimate—your own hand forming your own letters in a way that you've done since you were five years old. Thus, the brain is engaged in a slightly different way. When you are writing in your own handwriting, it's as if your soul is squeezing through your hand.

As soon as you have the urge to write something, write it down. If you hear a voice (yes, even if it sounds like your own mental processing!) or if you are compelled to form words or numbers or draw pictures, write these down.

Don't worry if you aren't able to write much—in general, you won't be as prolific working by hand as with laptop or computer; it's just the nature of the process. Conversely, don't worry if you receive so much that your hand can't keep up!

In writing by hand, your maximum output in one session, even for the most prolific writers, will be about ten pages. After that, your fingers will cramp, and you won't be able to maintain your attention.

Most folks will write a few pages. Some may write just one or two paragraphs. Whatever you write, regardless of quantity, is fine.

Keep writing for as long as you can, using the soft gaze. If you get distracted, or feel you can't hear your spirit guide, angel, or inner voice strongly anymore, take a breath and ask for clarification. You might say something like, "I can't hear you very well, please speak louder," or "Say that again, I missed it," or some other very normal phrase that you'd say to a friend who was speaking too quietly.

If you panic or get scared ("What am I doing? This is crazy! I can't hear anything!"), simply say to yourself that you are afraid, and allow this feeling to be answered.

As always, write what you receive, regardless if you think it is "right" or "good" or makes sense. Do not worry about how much or how little you write.

## Close the Channel

When you feel that you are finished writing (when you can't hear any more, you are having trouble staying focused, you're tired, you want to stop, or it's enough for the day), simply close the channel by saying, "I am closing this channel," bringing yourself out of trance, and opening your eyes. Just as with the laptop writing, put your journal away and go do something else. Don't read it, don't think about it, don't analyze or second-guess. Get out in this beautiful world and do something grounding and wonderful, like walking in the park.

Be in awe of what you have just done.

## How Often Should You Do Channeled Writing?

While I'd recommend channeling as much as you like, channeled writing either by laptop, computer, or hand is a different story. People seem to get tripped up on the information they receive. A little Divine guidance received in writing goes a very long way.

Plus, after you receive guidance, it's important that you take the time to act on it. For example, if during a channeled writing session your guides tell you to get a new job, you'll need some time to research job options. There really isn't a point sitting down to more channeled writing unless you've moved forward and acted on the guidance you've already received.

A rule of thumb: when you've done what you've been directed to do, then you're ready to go back for more guidance.

## Should I Save My Channeled Writing?

If you want to keep your channeled writing in leather-bound journals tipped with gold vermeil, that's your choice. I personally keep mine in my computer, and I almost never look at it—once a year, if that.

The way I see it is, the past is the past—it doesn't exist anymore. Once I've received and acted on Divine guidance, I'm ready to move forward. It doesn't make sense to rehash old news.

Another example? Say you've practiced yoga for the last thirty years. I don't suppose you need a recording of you doing every single yoga posture that you've ever done, in real time—"Oh look, here's me doing Downward Dog at age twenty-one, here's me doing it two days later," and so forth and so on, for the past three decades. What is important is that today you will do Downward Dog. You already have the information you gained from past practices of this posture. You do not need to review it again.

## Should I Share My Channeled Writing with Others?

Some of you will receive channeled writing that is specifically directed to the world. For example, The 33 Lessons are not personal instruction—I received clear guidance that these teachings would be disseminated to others without any stress and strain on my part, and that's exactly what came to pass.

When you receive this kind of writing—channeled writing meant to help the world—I highly suggest you share it. My belief is that the Divine is communicating through many of us at this time, and the more we share these messages, the more we can learn. If you like, you can send them to me via my website (www.sarawiseman.com) so they can be shared. I think we will be stunned to see how many people are receiving the same Divine messages at this time in humanity.

On the other hand, much channeled writing you receive will be personal—it is for your guidance only, and meant for your eyes alone. Just as you might pray and meditate in private, hold what you receive as personal information close to your heart.

# 14

⁓

# How to Use Divine Guidance

It's one thing to receive Divine guidance via channeling or channeled writing. It's another thing to know what to do with it. There is simply no point in channeling day and night, or filling up page after page with channeled writing, if you aren't going to take a close, hard look at what you received—and then act on it.

## Act On What You Receive

What I see happen to so many people is that they are so excited when they learn how to channel, they don't bother taking any action on what they receive. They don't make any changes, put any of this Divine guidance into motion—and after a while, the guidance stops coming. Their spirit guides, angels, or whoever they usually receive from get harder and harder to hear, and eventually, they can't be heard any more. These same folks, once gifted receivers, try to channel Divine guidance—but nothing arrives. At which point, these folks ask, "Why aren't my spirit guides giving me any new information?"

There's only one way to answer this question, and that's with another question: *Have you acted on the guidance they gave you?* If you keep asking to receive—but never act on what your guides tell you—after a while, they're going to stop responding.

Yep. Stop responding.

Imagine you had access to a Divine Dear Abby, who was more than happy to answer your question:

"Should I get my hair cut?"

"Yes, darling, get your hair cut."

Pretty straightforward, right?

But you're still not sure. So you write back every single day asking the same question:

"Oh, Abby, I just don't know if I should get my hair cut!"

"Yes, do it, you'll look great."

"But I'm not sure."

"Set up the appointment today!"

"But I love my long hair!"

"Do it!"

"But . . ."

And after a while, dear, Dear Abby will stop writing back. Why bother? You've ignored the last four messages she's given you.

Now, your guides won't be angry with you if you don't do what they say—there is no punishment, or sin, or morality in your direct connection with them. There is only compassion and love from their side. But they can't help you if you don't act on their guidance.

If you want real guidance:

1. Go to your guides as often as you need, but

2. Take their advice as Divine—and show your gratitude by acting on it.

Ask for clarification if you must, but don't ask the same question seven times. You'll hear the correct answer the first time—even if it isn't the answer you want to hear!

Remember: You don't have to do exactly what your guides say. Yes, they are there to help you, and yes, they are there to provide you with direction. But nothing says you *have* to do what they say. You have free will. You can take Divine guidance or leave it.

It's your choice.

## Listen, and Follow the Divine Guidance

Here's another common question: "Why don't my guides help me make day-to-day decisions?"

I'm sorry to tell you, but spirit guides are not particularly interested in the daily details and dramas of everyday life—what you should eat for lunch, what clothes to buy, where to go on vacation. They are interested in the bigger questions that will affect your soul growth, which may or may not include where to live, who to live with, what job to have, or questions to do with your health and spiritual life. These decisions can determine how you evolve and grow. But the little things . . . they don't really care. It's not important.

The problem is, sometimes these little things loom so large in front of us, it seems as if we're standing in front of a forest of details with our machete in hand, just trying to clear the path.

When you are struggling with everyday tasks, take a deep breath and, instead of asking for guidance on a specific aspect, just close your eyes, connect with the Divine and say, "Let me see clearly," or "Tell me what I need to know." Your angels have an innate ability to hack through all that daily detail and drama that looms in front of you, and they will do so instantly.

For example, say you're in a tizzy because you want to buy either a Toyota Prius or an Escape Hybrid, and you don't know which one. For some reason (why the world works this way I have no idea), you have to decide tomorrow or your financing deal expires. Tomorrow! So you connect with the Divine and ask, "Which car should I buy?" and you wait for a clear message to appear in your channeled writing: the letter *E*, for example, for Escape. Or *P*, for Prius. But there is no answer forthcoming from your guides.

Again, you ask the question. And while there is no answer about the car, you realize you are indeed writing something down: *Aunt Martha, Aunt Martha, Aunt Martha*. This is your great-aunt on your mother's side, and although she lives twenty minutes away, you have not seen in her in two years. "Go see Aunt Martha," you write.

What does this have to do with your car choice? Absolutely nothing! You slam your laptop shut and walk away, grumbling, "What kind of help are these angels, anyway? My financing is about to expire, and I still don't know what car to buy!"

However, the next day, as you are driving toward the Toyota car lot with your nearly expired financing letter firmly in hand, you pass the freeway exit that would take you to your Aunt Martha's. On a whim, you take it, and drive up to her tiny two-bedroom bungalow, complete with baskets of begonias hanging from the front porch. And there she is, older than you remember, cute as a bug's ear, wearing bright pink pants and the latest designer reading glasses. She invites you in for a cup of green tea (she's into health food), which you accept, and you sit there on the porch all afternoon, wondering why the heck you never visit her. In fact, you're having so much fun, you decide you'll let the car financing just slip away.

That's right, you decide you'll just let it go.

That evening, when you get home, your Aunt Martha phones you.

"There's one thing I forgot to mention," she says. "I can't drive any more, and I want you to have my car. Can you come over and take a look?"

You're surprised, but somehow not, when you head over the next day and there it is, sparkling in the sun. "It's last year's model, but it only has two thousand miles," she says, and you look at this perfect Toyota Prius, and smile.

If you tuned in right then and there, you'd hear your guides laughing away, delighted that you got what you wanted, but even happier because you *listened* and followed their guidance. There you were, all freaked out about what car to buy, and here the car you want is being given to you, for free.

When you follow Divine guidance, even if you don't understand it, things seem to fall into place.

## FOLLOWING DIVINE SIGNS, CLUES, AND STRANDS

When you're following Divine guidance, the most important thing to know is that usually, Divine guidance does not come to you all at once. Instead, it comes to you in pieces—in bits and clues and what I call *strands*. In most cases you will need to follow the strands you receive, until the next batch of information arrives.

To help people understand how this works, I like to use the example of a global positioning system (GPS). For those of you who haven't used this clever technology, you plug it into your car, key in the address you want to go to, and a little voice tells you which way to turn as you are driving.

How does it work?

It's magic!

Actually, I have no idea how it works, save for some newfangled technology having to do with satellites and little leprechauns living inside with tiny maps who shout out instructions as you drive.

You see, the GPS does not give you all the directions you need at once—there's no way you could absorb all that when you are driving. Instead, the GPS gives you small, very specific bits of information at a time; it tells you "turn right on Washington," and once you have done that, it tells you "turn left on Stark," and once you have done that, it tells you "go five miles on Wilson," and so on. Now, if you are the kind of driver that I am (and here I pause to let all my friends take a moment to laugh hysterically and be grateful they are not with me in a car at this very moment), then you might mistakenly turn left on Washington.

Hey, it happens!

At this point, the GPS will politely say something cryptic like "recalculating" or "readjusting." Readjusting to what? Why, to the new reality that "Hey, you sort of missed your turn there, bucko!" The GPS will calmly give you new directions from where you are now. Not where you were five minutes ago in the past, or where you'll be in the future, but Now.

Just like a GPS, the information you receive in channeling and channeled writing arrives a little bit at a time, and it always directs you to your right path from where you are Now.

What is your right path? The journey on which you will find the greatest bliss and love and joy in your life on this earth—and the greatest potential for soul growth.

Just as with a GPS, when you receive information from the Divine, you don't get all the directions at once. Once you turn right on Washington, you'll get the next direction. Once you turn left on Stark, you'll get the next direction. And so on. If you get lost, all you need to do is listen—and try again.

And even if you miss a turn (which most of us do frequently!) or even if you ignore clues and strands, your angels and spirit guides will continue to guide you; they will continue to nudge you in the right direction.

Finally, whereas GPS systems are fallible and sometimes don't get good reception or take into account unexpected construction zones in the middle of the highway, Divine guidance is absolutely correct. It may not be what you thought you'd hear ("Turn right on Washington? Really?") and it may not be what you want to hear ("But I don't want to turn right there!"). However, as you learn to listen and follow strands, you will soon see that the universe is guiding you on your path toward soul growth, one instruction at a time.

# 15

## How to Use Your Journal for Spiritual Growth

Many people have asked me if they can use their journals for Divine guidance—simply by writing in them, but without doing channeled writing.

Now, journal writing is a terrific tool for getting in touch with yourself, and knowing what you think; it's a superb method of clearing your head and clarifying your wants and needs. I myself have kept a journal since third grade, and almost all of the writers I know keep journals—there's nothing that feels as good as getting your inner thoughts down on paper! However, writing in your journal is not the same as receiving Divine guidance through channeling or channeled writing.

Journal writing is more similar to prayer, in which you ask the Divine, but you do not receive guidance in the same direct way. In fact, you could think of journal writing as praying on paper.

Is this a good thing? Absolutely!

Just remember that journal writing on its own won't give you the same type of guidance that channeling or channeled writing does. It's a terrific option, a powerful tool, another trick up your spiritual sleeve—but it's not exactly the same thing.

However (and this is important), writing in your journal takes quite a bit less *effort* than channeling or channeled writing, and some days, well, that's all you've got. You don't read *War and Peace* every night, do you? Of course you don't. Some days all you can manage is an episode of *Sponge Bob Square Pants*.

Am I comparing your journal writing to *Sponge Bob*? Of course not!

Some days, in fact many days, journal writing is much easier on the mind and heart than the intensity of channeling, and that's just fine. If you feel like writing in your journal, and this is an enjoyable practice for you, please do so, as often as you like!

Just don't expect it to provide you with the same type of guidance as the direct, two-way connection of channeling or channeled writing.

That clarified, let's talk about some of the best ways you can use your journal for spiritual growth.

## Recording Your Impressions

Most of you use your journal to record your impressions. This may take the form of a simple chronology of your day's events, writing down what's happened over the last few weeks, and so forth. You write what happened, who was there, how it made you feel, what you learned. It's a way of analyzing where you are right now, at this particular point on your life's path.

How can you expand this practice, and get more out of it? First, by paying attention to the tone of what you are writing. If you find you are mostly complaining, blaming others, everything is going wrong all the time, you're in a rut and so forth, dig a little deeper when you write.

If you're writing a stream-of-consciousness spewing, trying to get it all out on paper, and you find your journal entries are angry, miserable, depressed—it's time to take a look at what's going on.

If you are in a rut, have bad relationships, have money issues, are unhappy, are unhealthy, are overweight, drink too much, take too many pills, are ill, can't stop gambling, hate your job, whatever your issue is at this moment in time, it's time to stop writing about how miserable you are, and start praying for help.

And you can use your journal . . . to pray on paper.

## Praying On Paper

Those ancient scribes who copied prayers into thousand-page tomes had their heads filled with God all day long. This in itself was their meditation; as they wrote each word of scripture, the meaning of each word filled their bodies and souls like a mantra.

In this century, most of us don't copy holy text for ten hours a day with a quill pen. But you can receive the same benefits of prayer, simply by writing your thoughts as a prayer—and asking for help in what you are struggling with.

What's an example of how to pray on paper? In my life, here are some prayers I've written in my journal many, many times. "Oh God, please help me heal my relationship with this person." "Oh God, please protect my family." "Oh God, please provide enough money this month." "Oh God, please help my health to be strong." "Oh God, please show me the way." "Oh God, please help me know what to do." "Oh God, I'm totally confused, in so much pain, feel so alone, please, please, please help me." "Help! Please! Now!" And so forth. With the writing of these words, the Divine understands immediately what you need help with. Actually, they know it before you even write the words down. Yet, it is with the act of asking that they can begin to help you.

You notice that prayer on paper does not sound like, "Oh God, please make my evil boss move to the Bermuda Triangle and be swallowed whole by man-eating sharks and never be heard from again, so that I can take my rightful position as manager and earn a bigger salary, since I do all his work anyway."

This would not be an example of praying on paper.

Instead, what you need to do is

1. Identify the problem (e.g., you don't get along with your boss), and

2. Ask that the problem be solved in a way that is for the Highest Good.

Remember: You yourself don't know what the Highest Good is, and you also don't know what the solution is—otherwise you would have solved this problem already. The Divine knows the solution, you don't. Thus, all you need to do is request that the relationship be healed; the Divine will take care of the how.

Using your journal to pray on paper in this way is easy. All you need do is write the words down, and help is already at your side.

## Showing Gratitude

Just as you can ask for help in your journal, you can also say "thank you." This is also a form of prayer on paper—a cataloging of all the things that you are immensely grateful for.

Many of you have done this exercise before—listing twenty things that you are thankful for, fifty things, one hundred things. But doing this exercise one time is really not enough. Saying "thank you" to the Divine is something you can do constantly, at all times.

No amount of saying thank you is too much!

Every time you pray in your journal by writing down what you're thankful for, you create more of that beautiful, blessed, blissed out energy in your life.

Imagine that! Saying "thank you" brings you more of what you are thankful for, more of what you enjoy.

Quick, right now. Grab your journal, and write down twenty things you are grateful for. If you have more (and how can you not?) keep going.

Remember: *If you're not blissed out, you're not paying attention.*

# Dreams and Visions

Lots of folks keep a dream journal by their bed, and for good reason. Your dreams often bring you very clear information—visionary stuff—about where you're supposed to go and what you're supposed to do with your life.

For example, when I first began singing, I was often confused as to whether I should continue. I had no training, no background, certainly no previous indication of talent, and here I was, starting to sing at age forty-four. It was tough to believe that this was what I was supposed to do.

Luckily, the Divine intervened, bringing me two remarkably vivid dreams that gave me the answer.

In one dream, Ella Fitzgerald invited me up on stage with her, and when her bouncers tried to drag me off, she said, "No, this one stays up here," and began teaching me how to sing like she does. In my dream, I was singing like Ella, note for note!

A few weeks later, I dreamt that Jai Uttal, a pioneer in world music and a renowned kirtan singer, asked me if there was something I had forgotten to do in my life. In my dream, I answered, "I forgot that I wanted to sing." These dreams were huge, enormous, visionary—I woke up stunned that I'd had them.

The dreams were crystal clear, as real as life, and they left me with no doubt that I should continue on my music path. *If your dream is a Divine message to you, it will be very clear.* You will wake up with the understanding that the dream is a message—you will think, "I just received a message in my dream." While you are having the dream, you might find yourself thinking, "This is a message," or someone in your dream will actually say the words to you, "This is a message." You will remember these dreams clearly, and they'll be easy to interpret. They will in fact be difficult to misinterpret—and they will contain a vision or statement that you understand.

For example, Ella Fitzgerald saying, "No, this one stays up here" to *me*? That's pretty clear—it means I should get up on that stage and sing! Me telling Jai Uttal in my dream that "I forgot that I wanted to sing"? Those dreams helped me realize that singing is in fact a passion for me, and it's another way I channel—a voice flows through me from the Divine.

## Brainstorming and Creative Thinking

I started my writing career way back in the early 1980s as a copywriter in Seattle. Now, for those of you who might think this has something to do with copyright law, it doesn't. Copywriters are the people who write those catchy slogans for ad campaigns and persuade you to buy things you don't need. In the old days, copywriters wrote newspaper ads and what was called print media—back then, we sometimes called it junk mail. Nowadays, copywriters write a lot for the web—nowadays, we sometimes call it spam!

Whenever we had creative meetings at the ad agency, we'd use a technique called brainstorming to get our creative juices flowing. The idea is to throw out every idea you have—and I mean even the stupid, can't-possibly-work ones—and hopefully, through this process, come up with a good idea by 3:00 p.m., which was when the client was going to arrive at the meeting.

The whole idea of brainstorming is to banish negative thought. Just let that flow happen—because if you're so busy saying, "No, that won't work," you get all bottled up and your stomach hurts and your creative juices stop running. Instead, you basically "storm" your brain, throwing everything you can think of at it, looking at all the crazy ideas you can—especially the ones that won't work—in hopes of finding a solution.

Brainstorming is a perfect technique to use in your journal!

If you are a writer, artist, musician, inventor, scientist, or any other kind of creative person in any field whatsoever, you simply must have a journal or notebook in which to jot your creative insights. You simply must use your journal to brainstorm and write down all the ways you can possibly solve a problem.

Years ago, I took a class from a writing teacher who told me that "the answer lies in the pen." In other words, you don't know what your answer is going to be to a certain problem, until you write it down. Writing down fifty wrong ideas (brainstorming) ups the ante to nearly 100 percent that you're going to write down a right idea next.

It's my belief that people who work creatively (and this can be anyone in any field) always receive Divine guidance when they brainstorm. The Divine might not say, "Oh, by the way, here's the slogan for your next ad campaign." But in simply opening to the flow of the universe, you will channel answers.

Creativity? Soul growth? The source is the same.

## Using The 33 Lessons

There could be a book written on how to use your journal for soul growth, and there isn't time to cover that here. However, when you get to The 33 Lessons, you'll find the Divine is already one step ahead of us. Each Lesson is meant to be used with a journal—you read the Lesson, then you write your responses to specific questions. It's an incredible way to analyze your life—where you are now, and where you want to be.

Remember, all paths lead to the Divine. Channeling and channeled writing are one way. Prayer and meditation are another. Journal writing may work for you. And there are other methods not mentioned in this book—yoga class, hanging out in nature, serving in your community, being a great parent . . . There are endless ways to connect with the Divine.

It doesn't matter which path you take, as long as you are on *your* path. The Divine greets you, whether you travel by Toyota Prius, horse and buggy, on foot, or by hot air balloon.

The Divine meets you wherever you are.

# 16

—

# Manifesting:
# The Divine Approach

In certain circles, manifesting has become the mantra that rolls off our tongues the same way Nike's "Just Do It" tagline did years ago. *The Secret, The Law of Attraction*—these books have put manifesting in the spotlight and unlocked the key for plenty of people.

Yet, even though the way these books present manifesting is unique, manifesting itself is as old as the hills. Even Jesus taught it, with his famous "Ask and Ye Shall Receive" slogan.

Of course manifesting's popular—it sounds great! That whole idea of asking for what you want, then relaxing in your La-Z-Boy (or La-Z-Girl) as the universe brings it out on a giant silver platter right to where you're sitting? You don't even have to get up, or stop watching your big screen? What's not to like?

All your dreams realized—just because you asked for them!

All joking aside, this is in fact how manifesting works—*ask and you shall receive.*

However . . .

If you've ever seen the movie *Fantasia*, you know what happens to Mickey Mouse when he starts waving around Merlin's wand—a powerful magic wand he has no business holding. If you start acting like

Mickey, then everything you wave into existence with your magic manifesting wand becomes instantly available. And there you are, just like poor Mickey, running away from the animated army of your creations.

## What *Manifest* Means

To manifest doesn't even mean to create, although that's the way we commonly use it now. According to my nifty computer dictionary (Apple iBook) it means "to make something evident by showing or demonstrating it clearly." *To make something evident*—in other words, something that was there all the time suddenly becomes evident through manifestation.

It also means "to appear or to be revealed." Again, something that was there all the time suddenly appears or is revealed. It's not that it wasn't there before. It's that you suddenly notice it; you see it as being there for the first time.

And the most quirky definition of manifest—"to include something in a ship's cargo list," as in:

"Hey, what's in the hold of the *Salty Waters* today?"

"I dunno—let's check the manifest."

Once again, something that was already there (in the ship's cargo) is suddenly listed or tracked or called out so you know it's there.

By this time, you're starting to understand that manifesting does not create something new. Everything in the universe is energy, all energy endlessly flowing at all times. Nothing is ever new—not death, not birth, not even the things that seem new—because everything already exists, infinitely and endlessly. Manifesting simply calls into being (or into awareness) what was already there.

This is such a simple idea, it can be hard to grasp.

In the easiest terms, when you think of manifesting, consider this: whatever you want is already there. You just need to ask for it.

This isn't brain surgery—it's just Divine law.

# One Practice, Many Guises

New Age motivational speakers aren't the only ones hopping on the manifesting train. Remember goal setting? Remember five-year plans? Different words, same concept. Corporate leaders and business speakers taught manifesting long before the term hit the streets.

Understanding this makes it very clear that not all manifesting is spiritually based, and . . . drum roll here please . . . *it doesn't have to be spiritually based to work.* A lot of people use a basic, ego-driven style of manifesting that's pretty much the same as going to the mall with a brand-new credit card and saying, "Oh, I'd like this, and I'd like this, and this too," and pretty soon you're lugging around your purchases, a dozen bags and boxes in your arms, and yet you can't stop shopping. You're weighted down with stuff, your credit card is maxed out, and still you continue.

That's because manifesting works!

Why wouldn't you try to get more and more and more—more than you might ever need? It's entirely possible to overmanifest, the same way you can eat too much, drink too much, or do whatever it is that you do to excess.

People have known this for centuries:

*Ask and you shall receive.*

And the flip side:

*Be careful what you wish for, because you just might get it.*

## A Little Bit of Folk Wisdom

When my children were small, I used to read them fairy tales at bedtime—Brothers Grimm (which are grim indeed), Hans Christian Andersen, and other old folktales from around the world. I read these stories to them in part because when I was a kid I couldn't get enough of them—these hero's journeys, these cautionary tales, all designed to teach kids some universal truths about human existence and our collective soul.

One old German folktale goes something like this: A poor fisherman meets a magic fish who then grants him three wishes. At first the fisherman asks for simple things, but when his wife hears about the wish-granting fish, she gets angry and tells her husband to demand more—not a house, but a castle! Not a loaf of bread for dinner, but wheelbarrows of gold! And so forth and so on. You know where this is going. The fish gets disgusted and washes everything away, leaving the fisherman back in his little hut by the sea, with his wife weeping and wailing (and not a bit wiser) beside him.

A similar Swedish tale tells the story of a poor woodsman who gets three wishes from a tree fairy. He's hungry at the moment, so he wishes for a sausage. Voilà! There it is—a yummy sausage. He's pretty happy about the whole thing, until his wife (oh, how these wives get the short end of the stick in these stories) shouts at him for using his first wish so foolishly. He shouts back at her, "I wish that sausage was on the end of your nose." It's his second wish, don't you know? Of course that sausage attaches there as if with Super Glue. In the end, the woodsman valiantly uses his third wish to get the sausage off his wife's nose, and they eat the sausage for dinner.

The moral of these fairy tales:

*Ask and you shall receive.*

*Be careful what you wish for—you just might get it.*


## CREATE YOUR REALITY

I do believe we manifest our reality, as proscribed by *The Secret* and *The Law of Attraction*. However, I don't think that the occasional negative thought is going to throw the whole manifesting process into a tizzy, as some folks say. It's what we consistently dream about, work for, ask for, and bring into being that becomes our reality. Not the random thought, "I stink," or "I'll never make it."

I believe that the universe gives you a free pass on negative self-talk if it only happens now and then. It's when we become habitual with our self-doubt and self-loathing that the cosmos starts to follow what we believe. A slip-up now and then? Heck, we're human. By and large, most of us are doing the best we can do at this moment.

The Divine understands that some days we grow very, very slowly. Yet, we do grow.

This growing out of habits of negative thought and negative behavior is just like a kid who grows out of his sneakers every three months and needs a bigger size—it's all part of our soul growth. Over time, many of us will be able to move toward the habits of self-love and self-acceptance, and these positive thoughts will make up the bulk of our thought process. Louise Hay is famous for teaching self-love, and says on her DVD *You Can Heal Your Life* that self-love is one of the most important things we can do for ourselves.

However! We do not have to be 100 percent finished with negativity, grumpiness, pessimism, bad behavior, and so forth in order to move forward.

Do your best.

If you slip up, start over.

You do not wreck all your manifesting energy toward losing weight, for example, if you see yourself in the mirror and suddenly think, "I'm fat." Yes, it's a step back. But if you push that thought away and replace it with "I'm getting thin," or even better, "I love myself," there you are, right back in the flow.

Let me say this a different way: You don't have to have all your stuff worked out to make your life what you want. As you manifest, your life will change, and as your life changes, you'll change with it.

Let the small slip-ups go—and keep moving forward.

## What's On Your List?

In order to manifest successfully, we must be clear about what we want. Remember that definition, "to include something in a ship's cargo list"? That's what we need to do when we manifest. We put what we want on the list, and the next time we look in the hold, it will be there.

Why not ask for everything?

Have you ever overshopped for Christmas or another holiday?

In my family, we have a running joke when it comes to the holidays: "I'm cutting back this year," we all say. And then, Christmas Day comes and it's the same thing as the year before—way too much stuff!

When all the turkey or tamales or plum pudding or whatever it is you eat during the holidays has settled into your stomach, as you slump on the living room sofa surveying the wreckage—crumpled wrapping paper here, ribbon strewn there, gifts galore, with that horrible, horrible knowledge that your Visa bill is going to arrive in a few weeks . . . that's when you get a sick feeling of overload, or overconsumption, or just plain *too much,* and you realize that you didn't actually want that stuff anyway.

You just thought you wanted it. But now, you're not so sure.

The problem with manifesting is *it works.*

The problem with manifesting is that *we get what we ask for.*

The problem with manifesting is that sometimes *we ask for stuff we don't really even want.*

This is why I so strongly caution against manifesting if you aren't clear on what you do or don't want.

And even if you think you know exactly what you want . . . recognize that the Divine may have other plans that are far bigger, better, and more exciting than what you are thinking right now.

## The Myth of Materialism

Material things do not satisfy us. Never have, never will. While some New Age leaders say that it's fine to manifest extreme wealth, a gigantic house, or a luxury car, I don't believe this will make you happier. You'll get what you ask for, but you might not find it as attractive or appealing as you thought.

I grew up in an area of Seattle that was chock-a-block filled with rich people. Maybe they weren't the richest people in the world, but for Seattle during the 1970s, they were wealthy. A few blocks down the street from my house, there were mansions—acreages with lakefront property, docks and sailing boats, twelve bedrooms, servants, a kitchen for caterers, swimming pools, fountains in living rooms, and folks arriving in fancy cars and parties and tennis dates and golf tournaments and trips to Hawaii and Palm Springs and so on. Old-school, Seattle-style rich. Like a Pacific Northwest version of *The Great Gatsby*.

As a teen (not wealthy, not from a wealthy family, merely living down the street from wealthy people), I was often hired as a party helper—passing mini quiches and crab wontons on silver trays, taking coats to back bedrooms, freshening people's vodka and tonics. During the holidays, it seemed like those parties were nonstop. And what I began to notice was that some of these people who had absolutely every material thing they could want did not seem particularly happy.

They didn't seem to have a sense of purpose, or any awareness of their life's passion, or any kind of gratitude for their lives on this earth.

I saw this clearly with my fifteen-year-old eyes.

Some years later, I noticed something else. During the dot-com boom, many people had a sense of infallibility about money. But when the boom went bust, a state of panic ensued. The money might be going away. The Mercedes, the swimming pools, the mansions on the lake might be gone in a second.

Poof! Gone. See ya.

In recent years, as the global economy crashes and burns, we see this happening again.

Tell you what: it happens. Money comes, money goes, material things do the same. All of life is about constant change, endless flux; why should money and stuff be any different?

Enjoyment, not money, is the key.

Passion, purpose, fulfillment are the core.

Love, not stuff, is what will make you happy.

A sense of purpose in your life, waking up each day to realize you are here, and you are going to learn something new on this beautiful new day—this is what will make your life worth living.

So instead of manifesting a bigger house, manifest a better relationship with your spouse. (With divorce rates hovering at close to 50 percent for first marriages, according to a study by Rutgers University[5], I'd say we need some attention in this area.)

Instead of a great car, manifest a healthy, beautiful child who knows you love him or her.

Instead of wealth, manifest work that interests you, that you find captivating, that is useful to both you and the world.

In The 33 Lessons, the recommendation is consistently for three things: Connection. Compassion. Love.

I would guess that these are good things to manifest in your life.

*Connection. Compassion. Love.*

I would say there's a trifecta you can't go wrong with. A trio that, when you receive it, will delight your heart beyond all comprehension.


## How to Manifest Earthly Delights

Okay. Enough lecturing.

It's *not wrong* to manifest material things. Just make sure you know what you're doing—you might ask your spirit guides and angels first, "Will this make me happy, or make my life better, or be for the Highest Good?" And if your guides say no to that kayak or motocross bike or handbag that you just have to have, then consider skipping it.

This life is about soul growth, not filling up your garage with toys. Keep your eye on the real prizes—a peaceful and open heart, loving relationships, a connection to others, a connection with the Divine, and a life filled with purpose and passion—and you will save yourself a lot of distraction.

---

5  Rutger's University, The State of Our Unions annual report, 2007.

But what if you decide that you are ready to manifest some earthly delights: a few material possessions you've got a hankering for, some new standards of living, some achievements, some projects, some fame and fortune, some career goals you'd like to accomplish. Perhaps these are directly related to your work—your life's path and purpose. Perhaps it's just your preference; you really *do* want a big house, and you're pretty sure it's going to make you happy. You most definitely want a new car. You really do want that new job.

How do you manifest these into existence?

Well, frankly, it's about as easy as making a grocery list.

It should be harder, but it's not. It's just how Divine law works.

Remember that idea about calling something into existence? What you want is already there, right now. All you need to do is ask for it, and it will appear to you. You didn't create it. It was there all the time.

How?

Well, you already know how easy channeling is, and you also know that channeled writing is available to each of you as a tool for Divine guidance. Manifesting's right there in the same boat; everyone can do it.

Energy is Divine law. Everything exists all the time. If you want something, all you need to do is call it into your reality, your field of noticing. You do this with your thoughts.

It's so simple it's mind-boggling.

*If you want something from the universe, all you need to do is . . . ask.*

## How to Manifest In Writing

Using writing when you manifest is especially useful for most of us.

Why? It's the nature of the medium. When you manifest in your mind, you can forget what you manifested three weeks later. When you write it down, you can just look at the paper and see it right in front of you.

Writing also makes your intent crystal clear. It allows you to see precisely what you are calling into being. When you write something down, you can carry it with you, refer to it, adapt or change it if you need to. Whereas if you manifest in your head, things get muddy and cloudy and it's hard to sort everything out over time.

## Ground Rules of Manifesting

There's absolutely zero point in manifesting if you're going to shoot yourself in the foot. Thus, the rules of manifesting are:

**You can only manifest for yourself, not for others.** No matter how much you want your daughter to go to a good college and get a good job and be a good person on her life path, that is her manifestation, not yours. You can pray for your daughter. You can encourage her. But you can't manifest for her. You also can't manifest that your spouse gets a better job, or recovers from an illness, and so forth. You can only manifest for yourself.

**Understand what you are asking for.** Don't you have the feeling we've covered this point? We have. But it's crucial that you understand that not everything you ask for will make you happy, make you feel better about yourself, or contribute to your soul growth. In order to help you understand what you are asking for, please ask your guides and angels, "Is this something that I should manifest?" and then see what they say.

**Ask for the Highest Good, with no harm to all.** Manifesting harm to others is a really, really bad idea. Don't do it. No matter how much you hate your enemy (he's mean, she's a bully, he abuses you, she abandoned you, he's a backstabber, etc.), it's a tremendously bad idea to manifest that he or she will be attacked by a giant sea squid. First, you can't manifest for another person. Second, manifesting for harm is a dead-end street. Talk about the opposite of working on your soul growth! Talk about taking two, three, or fifteen steps backward on your life path!

Instead of manifesting harm to a person who is problematic to you, what you *can* do is manifest that you find a solution to your problem. Since you probably don't know what the answer is (or you would have tried it already), put this one squarely in the hands of the Divine: "I manifest that my problem with So-and-So (a.k.a. the Axis of Evil) is solved within three months for the Highest Good with no harm to all, and I am able to enjoy a peaceful relationship with him/her. I manifest that I will understand any changes I need to make. I leave the rest up to the Divine."

Another example: you've got a horrible, no-good, very bad boss. Instead of manifesting harm to her, manifest that a solution for your job problem arrives to you (a much better job, for example): "I manifest that I find the job of my dreams within three months, for the Highest Good with no harm to all, and that I understand clearly what I need to do to make this happen."

Even if you are manifesting for positive things, it's important to add that little caveat: for the Highest Good with no harm to all. It's boilerplate to the universe that says, "Hey, I've got good intention here!" Adding those nine simple words reminds you and the cosmos that you are working in the flow of light and love.

This is how all things move, change, and are manifested into being—within this flow.

THE UNIVERSE'S SCHEDULE MAY BE DIFFERENT THAN YOURS

Oh dear. This is where people get frustrated. "I manifested just like you said, but nothing happened," they say. No, nothing's happened . . . yet.

You might manifest that new job and ask that you'd like it to arrive immediately. Well, perhaps the universe, in all its infinite knowingness, understands quite well that you're not going to be ready for that new job immediately, because at this very moment, unbeknownst to you, your spouse has received a new job offer in a different state, and you're going to be moving. You might need three months to work through whatever it is you need to do—relocate, put in extra time with the family as your spouse deals with his/her new job—before your new job comes around. Or, perhaps, in the universe's infinite knowingness, the best new job for you is no new job. Perhaps what is required for soul growth is that you stay in your current job and figure out why you are making it crummy.

The universe knows.

Thus, all things come in their proper time.

## WHAT YOU RECEIVE MAY BE MORE THAN YOU IMAGINED

When I decided that I was ready to meet my partner, I manifested a man who was spiritual, kind, creative, and loyal. I knew spiritual topped the list, and I knew that the other characteristics were important, but I had no idea what order to rank them in. Frankly, they were all important! Knowing myself very well, I also wanted a man who would love my kids and have no children of his own or his kids would already be grown. I sat down, and I manifested my request. For the Highest Good with no harm to all. With the Divine in charge.

Now, you'll notice I didn't even bother to put in things like former male model, likes to give foot massages, able to ride a bike with no hands, etc. I certainly didn't put in what race, nationality, religion, or area of the world he lived in. I knew I didn't know enough to manifest those things. I wanted the Divine to guide me. If this man had the core elements that were important to me, I would be happy. I wanted to give the universe some leeway.

What happened next?

I met this man two weeks after I manifested him.

Did I recognize him?

Of course not!

I remember thinking, "That's a nice man" when I met him at the writing class at the coffee shop, but that was it. There was no instant spark of recognition. It wasn't until that fateful Prince concert months later, when I plowed into him in the crowded lobby, that I understood who he would eventually be in my life.

Talk about needing Divine guidance—it took a collision to clue me in!

And to my delight, this man wasn't just spiritual, kind, creative and loyal. He was much more. By letting the Divine choose for me, I'd found a man who not only matched me in the work I was doing at the time, but also in the work I didn't even know I was going to do yet.

Another example of letting the Divine choose is how quickly this book came into being. One day there was no book, no agent, no publisher. Yet two days after I said yes to channeling The 33 Lessons, the whole thing started moving; I received an agent, publisher, and book contract within three months. Door after door swung wide open, with a whole team of people inside saying "Welcome!" and "How can we help you?" as I stepped through in amazement.

This is because I choose to work in flow.

This is because I choose to let the Divine be in charge.

Anyone can work in flow—certainly not just me. This is Divine law, and all you have to do is accept it.

So, take it as a gift, a bonus, a great resounding yes! Life can be better than you even imagine, if you leave the universe a little wiggle room to provide for you in the most beautiful way. Thus, when you manifest, always ask for Divine help and guidance—and consider letting the Divine choose. You will not be disappointed. Working with the Divine, working in flow, will bring you far more than you could ever manifest (or even imagine) on your own.

# 17

⤙෴⤚

# Manifesting:
# The Practice

## Getting Specific

Figuring out the specifics before you begin to manifest is crucial. This takes some work and consideration on your part. Here, I've provided some examples of how you might do this.

Say you'd like to go on a vacation. You haven't been on a vacation for two years, and you really need a break. So, you begin manifesting. How do you do it?

Here's how I'd go about manifesting this (And I say to the universe, "Now, I don't need this particular vacation. It's just an example, okay!" That's how strong this Divine energy stuff is):

*I manifest a vacation to Hawaii for myself and my family within six months. Even though this trip will be expensive, financing is not a problem—I manifest that I will earn the money for this easily, or it will arrive from another source without any problem or difficulty for me. I manifest that we go to the island of Maui for two weeks, stay in a house on the beach, and have a wonderful time as a family. If another experience is better for me, I ask the Divine to please choose. I manifest this for the Highest Good, with no harm to all. Thank you.*

Do you see all the wiggle room I've left for the universe to do its Divine stuff? I've been specific as to what kind of vacation, by what time frame, and that the money part is taken care of. But I've also said clearly, "Hey guys, if you have a better option, I'm open to that."

Let's try another example.

Imagine you want a beach house. I live within forty-five minutes of the Pacific Ocean, and I've always wanted a beach house—so this time, I'm not going to say "for example only." However, even though I think I want a beach house, I actually don't know if having a beach house is in my best interest. I certainly don't want to get bogged down by a property that needs a lot of repair, or is outside my budget, or that I actually don't have time to visit very often. Thus, even though I think I want a beach house, I'm going to let the Divine take the lead on this one (frankly, my policy is to let the Divine take the lead on *everything!*). This is how I'd word this manifestation:

*I manifest a beautiful family beach house that's an easy distance from where I live now—it's a safe drive and is very accessible to me. I can get to it often enough for a quick weekend visit. This beach house has plenty of room for my family and friends. It's situated within a protected area, such as on a waterfront bay or river that flows to the sea, and is safe from tide and storm. It's an easygoing place with a big front deck or porch and is nestled in sandy dunes. It needs very little repair and is easy to maintain. It has a wood stove in case the power goes out. I can afford it easily, or it arrives to me as a gift or through some other effortless source. I manifest this beachhouse to arrive to me within three years from today. I manifest this through the Divine, only if this is within my best interest. If there is another possibility that I cannot yet imagine, I ask for this, or whatever the Divine has in store for me. I request the Highest Good and no harm to all. Thank you.*

Do you see how specific I was about the dunes, the front porch, the protected area? That's because I have already *seen* this beach house in my mind's eye. I could draw you a picture of it, right down to the floor layout. That's one reason I think this beach house is something that is going to come into my field of view fairly soon, because I've already seen it.

Now, in looking at how much beach houses currently cost, I gasp in shock—there's no way I could afford that! Even the most dilapidated fixer-upper costs more than I could pay. And yet, this is a place that I have seen in my mind's eye. But because there are some things that are definitely unclear (having enough time to have a beach house; what appears to be an impossible cost), I ask for the Divine to choose. Within three years, this will have come to pass in whatever manner that is best—and I will delight in the surprise that it brings.

When you write your manifestations, you don't have to use my wording. But be specific in the same way I've been in my examples. Add in lots of wiggle room—you don't know what the Divine has in store for you, and if you are choosing to work in flow, you can count on it being better than you can imagine.

If you can already *see* a vision of your manifestation, you're very close to having it come forth for you. Remember, you don't create your manifestation; it exists already. It exists even now, even before you've started to think about it.

## Timing Your Manifesting

You know when you send an email to someone and you add an attachment? Well, the most effective way to manifest is to "attach" your manifestation to a session of channeling, channeled writing, meditation, or prayer. Why? Well, by now you should know that when you're connected with the Divine in any of these four activities, you'll be in flow. What's flow? It's when you're right there, the energy of the universe pouring through you, working with your guides and angels, in direct connection with the Divine.

Flow is where you want to be when you manifest.

## Checklist for Manifesting

As you think about what you're going to manifest, keep this checklist handy:

1. Set a time limit for when you would like this to be created (in a month, etc.).

2. Set out the specifics of what you want—almost as if you're making an exact description of what you are calling into being. It's that old cargo list of what's in the ship's hold. If you want three chickens and six boxes of gunpowder to be in the ship's hold next time you look, then write 'em down. You can be as detailed as you want, or you can keep it fairly loose on the details that you're not fussy about.

3. Ask for the Highest Good.

4. Ask for no harm to all.

5. Ask the Divine to choose for you—remember that your guides and angels may have other, better, more wonderful plans that you haven't even thought of yet.

6. Say thank you.

Still not sure how to write it? Here's another example.

Imagine you have a book of poems that you'd like to be published. You're not in it for the money; you'd just like your poems to be read. Here's how I'd manifest that:

*I manifest that my book of poetry is published within one year, and that it enjoys an appreciative audience. I manifest this for the Highest Good, and no harm to all. I ask the Divine to guide me.*

Now, you'll notice in this case that I'm not overly specific. I didn't say published by a traditional publisher, in fact, I leave it very open that this book of poems might be self-published. If you didn't want to self-publish this book, you'd need to be very specific: *I manifest that this book of poetry is accepted by a publisher within one year and be published at their next scheduled printing.*

## Practice Manifestations

Try a few practice manifestations of your own here—choose three things you'd like to manifest, small or large. Then write them down.

1. Manifest something small here, for practice only.
2. Manifest something medium here, for practice only.
3. Manifest something huge here, for practice only.

Even though it seems counterintuitive, it's not one bit harder to manifest something "big" than it is to manifest something small. This can be hard to understand, but it's just Divine law. You don't need more energy to create something big. You simply need to work in flow.

## Manifesting, the Real Deal

A few minutes ago, you wrote down three practice manifestations, to get the hang of it. Now, you're going to do the real thing.

First, set yourself up in the same type of space and place as you did for channeled writing. Use your computer, laptop, journal—whatever's most comfortable for you.

You know the drill: curl up cozily wherever you are, make sure you have privacy, and make sure there aren't any electronic interruptions. Start off by entering into a light trance: close your eyes. Breathe in through the nose, out through the mouth, breathe deeply into your belly.

As you begin to sense the presence of your spirit guides or angels, invite them to become more apparent, by saying, "Angels come to me," or whatever other phrase you like.

Say a short prayer, out loud or in your mind, such as, "I am going to manifest some new things in my life, and I ask for your guidance and assistance. I also ask for the Highest Good and no harm to all. If you have other guidance for me or want me to move in a different direction, please make this easily apparent to me."

If you find yourself too tranced out, simply request that you bring yourself out of trance to a state of greater awareness. If you find yourself too distracted, simply ask that you go in a tad bit deeper. Now, open your eyes, and in this relaxed, just-at-the-edge-of-trance state, start writing your manifestations.

*I manifest this, in this time frame, with these specifics, with the Highest Good and no harm for all.* If you have already *seen* what you are calling forth, use this pre-sight to fill in your specifics (for example, as I did with the dunes and front porch for the beach house).

Once you've manifested the first thing you want, manifest something else.

*I manifest this, in this time frame, with these specifics, with the Highest Good and no harm for all.* And so on.

There isn't any limit as to how much you can manifest. But, as your list gets longer, continue to check in with your guides and ask if this is in your best interest, or if they have any better suggestions.

If your guides have something to say, believe me, you will hear from them!

*I manifest this only if it is in my best interest from the Divine. I accept this manifestation or I welcome something different, something bigger or better that is beyond my imagination at this time.*

Now, finally ask for a sign that you will know this manifestation has happened (you'll learn more about how to read and interpret these signs soon).

Simply write, *I ask for a sign that this manifestation is in process or has been moved into my awareness.*

Stay in a trance for a while after you have finished with your manifestations. Enjoy this state! Say "thank you" to the Divine for this beautiful life, and for what you have just manifested to come into your awareness. When you are ready, return to this awareness.

That's it! You've just completed the first stage of manifesting! It's exciting, and you're going to enjoy seeing what happens soon.

If you want to, keep these written manifestations in a safe place. Some people like to have them available to look at, some like to keep them in a private drawer. Look at them now and then—monthly, weekly, or daily if you like. Or don't look at them at all. It really doesn't matter. The energy is already in motion.

## The Second Stage of Manifesting

In order for you to call your manifestation into reality, you also need to do something else besides write it down. You need to act as if your manifestation has already happened, is in the process of happening, or is just arriving to you at this moment. You need to stay in flow.

For example, say you have manifested a necklace to wear to an upcoming event, and you want something really special and unique. You've manifested that you're going to find this necklace in the next two days, and even though you're worried that it's going to be expensive, you've manifested that it will come to you without any financial strain. You've put in your request to the universe, and the universe is working on it.

However, you need to do your part to keep the energy flowing. What this means is that anything you can do to work toward getting closer to this particular piece of jewelry is going to be useful. Some ways to stay in flow might be to visit shops or estate sales where they sell jewelry, look in catalogs, or browse the Internet.

Staying actively in flow helps the Divine move things along. Focus on this necklace, as if you've got a big magnetic beam in your brain, and let yourself be attracted to it, and it to you.

Whatever you do, don't write down your manifestation and then climb back into bed, pull the covers over your head and say, "There, that's taken care of; my job's done!"

No. If you want manifesting to work, you must

1.  Write down what you want, and

2.  Continue to keep the energy moving by staying in flow via your actions.

In the case of the necklace, this might seem difficult. "How can I know what I'm attracting if I don't even know what it looks like?"

Ah, but you do. Remember, this necklace already exists. Thus, all you need to do is listen ever so carefully to the guidance the Divine will send you.

For example, maybe you get a hunch that you might find this necklace at an estate sale. On the drive there, you hear the words, "turn left" in your ear. Of course, you turn left. This is following strands. Suddenly, you spy a small secondhand shop that you've never noticed before. It's not the estate sale, of course, but you definitely feel you should stop. So you do. This is being in flow. You walk in, rush to the jewelry case, and there it is—your necklace. The tag's unmarked, and as you take it trembling to the counter, you're sure it's going to be too expensive.

"There's no price marked," you offer.

"The owner's at lunch," the salesperson answers. "How about twenty dollars?"

You hand her the bill and walk out the door in a daze, necklace in hand.

Now . . . if you hadn't been headed to that estate sale, you wouldn't have heard the message to turn left, and thus wouldn't have gone into that secondhand store, and you wouldn't have found your necklace.

You've got to follow strands and be in flow, and be willing to go where the Divine leads you.

Here's a final example of how you need to put your energy toward what you want to manifest. Let's say you want to be a mystery writer. I mean, you really want to be a mystery writer.

But nothing happens.

Then you realize, you can manifest this. And so you manifest: *I want to be a mystery writer who writes ten popular books in a series that is published by a traditional publisher, and I want my first book to be picked up by an agent within one month of completion, and accepted by a publisher within four months after that. For the Highest Good, no harm to all.*

Okay, this is brilliant manifesting, but now it's time to get started putting your energy in flow.

The first step, of course, is to write your mystery. Yep. You gotta write the book, do it right, and if you don't know how to write it at the level of the market, you need to learn how. Once that's done, you need to figure out how to sell it to an agent. Both of these are big tasks, with huge learning curves. As you're thinking about how to stay in flow, you get a postcard in the mail advertising a local writer's conference—should you go? Of course you should! At the conference, you meet an agent who specializes in mystery novels. Should you send your book to him when it's done? Of course you should!

Without action, nothing happens.

Without following strands and staying in flow, nothing happens.

## The Third Stage of Manifesting

The third stage of manifesting is to accept gifts as they appear.

When you manifest a new job, put your energy into finding that job, and then that new job appears to you—the next step is to accept this job as a gift from the universe.

If you manifest that you will become a famous mystery writer, and you work feverishly and nonstop to make this happen, and it happens—then you accept this gift from the universe.

# How to Follow Signs, Clues, and Strands

After you manifest, Divine guidance will begin to arrive—signs, clues, and strands that help you know where to be active and how to stay in flow. The Divine communicates with us in many ways besides channeling and channeled writing, including:

**Written words:** Street signs. Road signs. Freeway signs. A piece of paper fluttering by on the street. A message in a bottle that you discover on the beach. Business cards, brochures, a phrase from a book you pick up in a bookstore, an article you read on the Web, seemingly at random. All of these may be clues or strands that you can follow.

**Electronica:** Songs on the radio and ads on TV are common ways the Divine reaches us. You might hear a phrase that catches your ear, and you know it's important. Or a strange phone call or email might come in unexpectedly. You don't understand why it's important, but you just know it is.

**Repeated messages:** If you hear a name or word or phrase in a conversation, and then you see it in a book the next day, this name is probably important. Pay attention to random things that come in multiples in a short period of time, and follow up on them. For example, if I heard the same name a few times, I might Google the name to see what shows up. It might be nothing—or it might be the next step on my path.

**Synchronicities, coincidence, happenstance:** That long-lost friend you were just thinking about the other day and then ran into on the street today? That's synchronicity. The car accident you were in that caused you to go to the doctor, and while in the doctor's waiting room you met the new business partner you'd been searching for? That's synchronicity. Being aware of synchronicities and paying attention to where they lead you is a way to work in flow.

**Unexpected sources:** Checks in the mail, surprise inheritances from the great-uncle you never knew you had, money found in a wad on the street. These are some examples of unexpected sources. Others might be letters from people you don't know, a call from a head-hunter, and so forth.

**Surprises:** Surprises are surprises! These are things that make you gasp and swoon with delight, and make you immediately say a prayer of gratitude to God. Accept them. Open them. Enjoy them. They are gifts to you from the Divine.

## Changing What You've Manifested

At any time, you may change what you are manifesting, or what you have already manifested. However, the timing can get tricky.

Once something's been put in motion, it's hard to stop—think of a snowball rolling down the hill, gathering speed and mass. For example: Let's say you've manifested that new job, and have put your energy toward making it happen. You've sent resumes, made contacts, filled out applications. And then, just as you're buying a new outfit for the big interview on Monday, you get the news: You're getting a big, fat raise with the company you already work for. It isn't a new job; it's the same position. But you get more money, and a slightly better office space.

This can get tricky, because you've already manifested a new job. Thus, it exists, even if you can't see it yet. It's making itself known to you soon, even if you're no longer sure you want it.

When a choice is presented to you like this, it can be confusing. Which is the right decision? It's the proverbial fork in the road. Turn left? Turn right? You have to choose, and even with help from your guides, it still may not be clear which path is the better one to take.

Is there a wrong decision? There might be.

Is there a right decision? There might be.

Are both decisions equal, and either way you go is fine? Quite possibly.

Often, these very difficult decisions are the ones we look back at and say, "That decision changed my life." We don't know which way to go, we try to hear our guides, and we move in a direction, right or wrong, and our lives are changed completely by our action.

My advice in this situation?

When energy is moving and you're unsure what to do, get out of the way and try to figure out where the flow is. Ask your guides to help. Ask them again. When in doubt, just say yes to what's happening, even if you don't understand it. Energy brings more energy. Whatever you do, even if you're not sure why, or how, or what, stay in flow. The universe, in an infinite and endless state of manifestation, is bringing forth what already exists.

If you've manifested one thing and end up changing your mind, as in the case of the job, you certainly might expect to receive both things—the raise at your current job, plus an offer for the job of your dreams—and these might show up fairly near the same time, within a few hours or days of each other.

Sometimes you have to choose.

Sometimes, even with the best intentions, even when you are working in flow, you have to walk blind.

## Walking Blind

An artist friend of mine, Layne Young, uses the term *walking blind* to describe what happens when you don't know where you're going—but you still keep moving forward.

Once you've manifested something, signs, clues, and strands begin to arrive, but they may not be clear. For example, you might hear the name Marilyn in a conversation, and then see the name Marilyn in a book, and then you might pass a poster of Marilyn Monroe in a shop window. You don't know how Marilyn relates to the new job you've manifested, but then when a company calls you for an interview, the interviewer says her name is Marilyn.

You merrily go to the interview with the woman Marilyn, sure it's a shoo-in. But as it happens, you are not offered the job.

What's going on here? Wasn't the name Marilyn a sign? Didn't you follow all the Divine strands? Didn't you stay in flow?

You drive home dejected, wondering why it didn't work. And while you're driving, you happen to catch the tail end of a news item on the radio about a new company that's just come to town. It's not called Marilyn Company or anything—that clue or strand has already been used. But because you walked blind, because you followed all the various Marilyn clues, here you are in the car—the right place at exactly the right time—when this news story came on.

You call the company up the next day, and yes, they're hiring. Four days later, they hire you.

This is an example of how to walk blind—using all the universe's clues or strands, but not worrying too much if you can't see what's going on.

Just keep walking.

That example's pretty straightforward. But when you are on a bigger project, or a bigger quest, such as a project or task that takes a lot of time and has a lot of elements to it (such as writing a book, opening a business, moving to a new city, raising children), you need a lot of help from the Divine! And so you have to listen and look very carefully for possible clues and strands, even if you aren't sure what they mean.

I can't tell you how many wrong turns I've taken as I walked blind on my life's path! Yet, I am following Divine guidance the best that I can. You'll follow as best you can, too. That's all we can do. If something is important to your soul growth, the Divine will continue to show you, over and over, until you get it.

And yes, it can be very difficult to walk blind. Following signs and synchronicities and strands can be confusing, especially when they go against logic and so-called common sense.

Do it anyway.

What happens if you do get off the path? What happens if you ask for Divine guidance and you still don't know what to do? What happens when you're totally lost, and nothing you've manifested seems to be happening?

This could mean:

- Your time frame is not the Divine's time frame.

- This manifestation may not be in your best interest.

- You're still missing key signs and symbols—look again, especially right under your nose.

- You're not following up with direct action and energy flow toward this manifestation.

- Something different is on its way.

- This is a manifestation that actually no longer interests you or is no longer required by you. You've outgrown it.

## When What You Want Changes

As your soul growth continues, you may not want what you have previously manifested, or even what you are now in the process of manifesting. Let's say that you've been manifesting for years that you want to be rich, have a mansion, and have a happy family life. Those are three things you want. Now, as it happens, you are blessed with an extremely joyous family life. You still have trouble paying the bills, and your house needs a new roof that you can't afford, but you just love your family and they love you back.

Pretty neat, huh?

At some point, while you are manifesting getting filthy rich and having a giant mansion with a five-car garage and working actively in flow to make this happen, you achieve some soul growth. And suddenly it hits you: you don't actually care about being rich, or having a mansion. You are so blessed, so happy, so blissed out with your family life that you don't need a single other thing in your life to make you happy. You're content, you're at peace, you're grateful, and every day you say "thank you" for such a beautiful life.

What you thought you wanted is no longer meaningful for you. What you once wanted is no longer required.

If this is the case, simply stop putting your energy into what you have manifested. The universe knows. With soul growth, as you become closer to what is Divine, and as you follow Divine guidance more closely each day, your need for manifesting tends to ease up.

*You become happy with what is.*

Even though your roof still leaks and your bills still stack up, you don't seem to mind anymore. It's just not important. You become a person who is aligned with the Divine, who frequently feels bliss, who has an open heart, who is actively involved in the flow of the universe. You begin to understand that all of life is transitory, ceaselessly changing. You begin to understand what makes you truly happy— what The 33 Lessons lists as Connection. Compassion. Love.

Because you are so closely aligned with the Divine and you follow Divine guidance instead of your own ego, your need for manifestation becomes less and less. Mostly, you're happy to go with Divine will, wherever that leads.

Mostly, you're just happy to be here, in this life.

This is the most blessed and blissed state to be in.

I recommend that while it's important that you know how to use manifestation as a tool—more often than not, you let the Divine choose for you.

How to do this? For example, if you are having trouble with money, you might manifest: *I'm having a problem with money. I'd rather focus on my work in this world, rather than worry about bills. I manifest that I am free from worries about money, and I ask for Divine help with this. For the Highest Good, no harm to all. Thank you.*

Then, watch for signs and symbols to show that this has happened. Stop worrying about money. Know that you're working in flow, and the Divine is in charge. You will be continually surprised at what is manifested by the universe, when you allow the Divine to choose.

## Using Manifesting for Soul Growth

You now understand how to manifest in a way that supports your soul growth. You understand that you have the option of asking the Divine to choose, and that you may enjoy your life more than you thought possible if you choose this path. You understand that you must put energy behind your manifestation in order to bring it forward—you must work in flow. You understand how to follow clues and strands, and why it's okay to walk blind. As you use these skills in your life, you will be amazed at how quickly your life becomes transformed.

Next, as you read The 33 Lessons, you will understand even more fully how present the Divine is, at all times, in all aspects of your life, and how this sublime energy is always, endlessly available to you.

PART TWO

# The 33 Lessons

# Preface

ONE AFTERNOON IN MARCH 2008, I was at home organizing books on a new bookshelf. This might not sound like a big deal, but it was to me—for nearly three years, due to the distractions of family and work and life, my personal library books had been boxed and stacked in the basement. Now, after half a day of sawing and drilling, I had a new bookshelf, and I was tremendously excited to rip open those boxes and put my beloved books in their rightful places.

Opening the first box, I was surprised to find Doreen Virtue's *Divine Guidance* right on top. I paused for a moment, and considered. For the last few days, I'd heard or seen the name Doreen Virtue almost everywhere I went—in an email, overheard in conversation, read in a magazine article, and mentioned to me by a friend.

I knew this was a sign, a strand, that I was supposed to follow. However, I was confused: this particular book was one I'd read many times. Why would I need to read it again?

As I picked up the book to look closer, I heard a voice in my right ear: "We want you to write this," the voice said clearly.

I stood stunned, holding the book in my hand.

"Doreen Virtue?" I stuttered. "But she writes about angels."

"We want you to write this," the voice repeated. "Using writing."

I didn't know what to say. I was in the middle of writing my third novel, and I had no plans to stop. What's more, I didn't know anything about angels—I'd never even seen one.

"But Doreen Virtue is . . ." I stammered. "Doreen Virtue does . . ." I didn't know how to express how important I thought her work was, and why I couldn't possibly write like that.

The voice didn't let me finish. "We want you to teach this."

I waited.

"We want you to write this and teach it. Using writing."

It was pretty clear that I was being given Divine guidance. And even though I don't know much, I did know enough not to argue.

"Okay," I gulped. "But I don't know anything about angels or . . . whatever it is you want me to write. You'll have to tell me what to say."

Have you ever heard a collective nod?

That's what I heard that day.

When Saturday morning came, I showered, dressed, drank my coffee, and paced nervously—my hands were actually shaking! I knew what was next, even though I hadn't done channeled writing in years.

I was going to sit down and receive.

"I don't know what this is, but I'm ready," I finally said, then plugged in my laptop, closed my eyes, and listened. Constance arrived to me immediately, and with her came The 33 Lessons.

I took "dictation" from Constance, Miriam, and Gabriel almost every morning for the next two months. I sat in session as long as I could and sometimes received two Lessons in one sitting. Sometimes they were long, sometimes they were short. Every time I sat, they arrived.

I dealt with my fears and confusion as best I could, as well as the exhaustion that the process sometimes brought on. (As you'll come to know, it takes a lot of focus to receive.)

During this time, I didn't think about what I was doing, why I was doing it, or what would happen afterward. I knew my job was to simply show up to the task of receiving, and that is what I did.

Here, The 33 Lessons, as I received them, as a message to the world and to whoever seeks them.

# Introduction

## CONSTANCE

NEVER BEFORE HAVE WE IN this realm been able to use the methodology of writing as a tool to reach so many people. The advent of electronica has also made this connection easier. Even now, people use electronica to pour their heart out to the universe. They are manifesting even as they send their tales to the ethernet. Do you notice we say ethernet? It is not the Internet that you manifest into, it is the ether—the cosmic consciousness, the universal Now.

Much of this connection is still vile. Like traders in the temple, many of you are selling things in holy space, bartering addiction. Pornography, this is a black vibration, the place that needs the most curing for so many of you. Pornography can never allow you peace; it is a grasping and excitement for what can never satisfy. There is no satisfaction in it; it is not possible. Drugs and addiction are also just a masking of your heart breaking, of crying out for God, for the help of your angels. It is a numbing down so you do not have to feel.

But we say to you this: You can feel. You will be safe with us. First you must call upon us, as direct emissaries of God. Direct emissaries, we say, and in fact, there is no division. We are God, we are One as are you. It is all the same. Surely, you know this? You are the same with your brother, with your parent, with your enemy, with your child, with your husband or wife or boss, or the most evil person you can imagine. This is no new story. We are one soul, in many places and forms. One Divine God as All.

It is confusing to you, because in your own mind you have what you call the ego, or the I, me, mine, or what we prefer to call a separate self, or earth self. This makes you believe that you are different or separate from God. Over time, as your soul growth continues, this separation will become less apparent to you.

You must know that it is possible to lock into the hum and feel the consciousness of the universe at all times. There are enlightened beings on Earth who do this, and some of them you have seen, and some of them you know by name. There are others, so many others, who work silently in a much smaller way, and hear the voice of God directly in their minds, and speak the voice of God directly with their lips. We say to these: we see your works.

For these Lessons, you will have three guides, Constance, Miriam, and Another to arrive later, and we will divide the Lessons in a way that you can understand them.

Again, we remind you that not everyone starts from the same place, and there are some limits of understanding that must be addressed before we can begin with all people. This is of no matter.

Transformation comes to all in time. It is simply a matter of when.

For you, the one who receives. This book will be completed rapidly and will not be long. It is meant to be easy for you to use and learn. We present things to you in a form, because we want this word to become available. We will distribute this to those who need it; there is no concern for you there. You will be guided entirely and will know what to do with this work when it is done. The only thing you must do is to come and take our notes and teachings. We know already you will do this, you have asked to be a scribe, and we welcome your service with gladness.

We are all One. There is no more important journey than the growth of the soul.

# The purpose of life is soul growth.

~

## CONSTANCE

THE PURPOSE OF LIFE IS soul growth. We are here to become transcendent and to become one with God. There is no more to life than this.

In other words, we are here to love.

Surely, you know this?

But what makes it difficult for people to love is that their tender hearts have been injured so many times; they have been heartbroken, betrayed, caused immeasurable suffering. You can have your heart broken by poverty, by evil, by decadence, by neglect and inattention. As now we see in your entire society: violence, anger, abuse, war, hatred, pornography, molestation. These are all things that must end.

You must ask yourself, to not allow these things within your culture.

You must choose the force of peace.

Please gather a journal. Or if you prefer, please use another writing device. We ask that you find a quiet, private, uninterrupted space that you may be in by yourself for a time. We understand that you have concerns of time, and we ask you, why do you allow this? Time is of no importance. Life extends unto old age, or life is ended in a breath. You do not know which, and these are the same. Just be, in your life. But surely you know this already?

For the first Lesson, you will sit quietly, with your writing implements near and you will count slowly, in your mind backwards from ten to one. During this time, you will breathe in through your nose, deep into the belly, and allow the breath to come out naturally. This is how we will breathe. This simple breath may be hard for many of you, and it is designed to seep into your heart. Please, attend with us.

## Exercise

We now ask that you write of the most heartbreaking moment in your life. We do not provide a list of tragedies, sufferings, a catalog of personal pain. Such a list will not be of use to those of you who understand what pain is.

We ask that you begin at the beginning, and you write down the details of this personal tragedy, this personal suffering, until you are done.

If you have had a particularly troubling time for a number of years, we would like you to take only one specific memory, situation, or argument, and write this memory.

If you are numb to the pain, we ask that you consider: what do you most avoid?

Breathe in deeply, and call on us for courage by saying, "Angels, give me courage."

Even if you do not believe, please say these words.

Breathe out, and begin to write.

Every time you come to a pause, or a difficult point, close your eyes, breathe in and picture the situation again in your mind.

This will be painful. We are here, call us around you!

Do not worry about the Truth. The Truth will arrive in your writing of this incident. Concentrate only about sitting down, breathing, and using your writing implements to record this painful incident in your life.

When you are done writing, you may ask for forgiveness. You may ask to forgive. You may ask to be released from your anger. You may ask for atonement. You may ask for help. You may ask for whatever you feel the need, or for what you need but do not know the name of.

We are with you always, all of us together without separation or difference, all One. We do not abandon you, just as the body cannot abandon its heart, or its brain, or its lungs. We do not abandon you; we are an eternal, everlasting, infinite Divine body.

# Consider your position.

ᴦ

## MIRIAM

In this Lesson we ask that you consider your position. We here are of the angelic realm, and do not concern ourselves with material possessions and collaborations. They are as dust on the wind.

We ask that you consider your position, in writing. We are not concerned if you are a good writer, a bad writer; there is no such thing as this in our definitions. Each writing is marvelous and enchanting to God. Every writing reaches the infinite consciousness. Thus we are not concerned with the style of writing you choose to employ when you write in these Lessons. We ask only that you return to us each time you are called.

How will you know when you are called?

You will, my child. You know this already, as do you, and you, and you. Even you, the skeptic, the nonbeliever, even you know this. When you are called, we ask that you come. We will call you and you will hear us.

Many of you hear us already through signs in the air, a brushing feeling upon your shoulder, a shimmering on your skin. Some of you feel us as Truth, as a chill that runs along your spine.

We often come in the form of recognition—you may feel this chill down your back when someone tells you something that you know is True.

We often speak to you through the energetic forms and the ethernet. This is a place where is it easy for us to work within vibrations.

## Exercise

We ask that you consider your position. In your world, on earth, we ask that you answer these questions, in writing.

1. What is your income?
2. What are your debts?
3. How many items of clothing do you have?
4. How much food do you eat?
5. How much do you spend on giving of alms?
6. How much work do you do for your survival?
7. How much work do you do for the good of others?
8. Are you a parent?
9. Do you care for others?
10. Do you care for the aged?
11. Do you pray?
12. Do you meditate?
13. Do you sing?
14. What time of yours is spent in obsession and fantasy?
15. What addictions are owned by you?
16. Do you have proclivities that make your heart sad?
17. Do you have a temper?
18. Do you commit violence?
19. Are you kind to animals?
20. Are you kind to children?

And now, dear ones, we ask that you call on us, and that you spend time in connection, as before. Breathing in the nose, breathing into the belly, letting the air exhale deeply out the nose. Close your eyes, and consider these questions, and what you have answered. And when you are ready, open your eyes. And write what occurs to you, about a particular answer you have been given.

We do not choose which questions will be of interest to you. We know that one will prompt you to write further.

Again, do not worry about the Truth. Write only the details. The Truth will arrive as a great shining light when it shines.

Do not worry too much, either, about lying.

There is no lie too big for the Truth.

There is no lie too big for God.

## LESSON THREE

# A new literacy of the soul.

## CONSTANCE

As WE HAVE TOLD YOU, this volume is being dictated by three. Three beings from the angelic realm: Constance, who will dictate to you most of the information; Miriam, from whom you will learn Truth; and Another, who will arrive later.

We are the ones sent to do this task, this particular volume. Others will connect with others. The world is being filled with this same word.

Within the new literacy, we have a new literacy of the soul.

This is for what we have come.

Soul growth. In which you become transcendent, and in which the earthliness of the world no longer intrudes, attracts, or causes pain or confusion. In which you rise up and become One. This is the goal of each life, in the time that you have in your body.

There is the popular idea that you must be salvageable. Yet this is fallacy. You are saved already. All beings are saved. There is no salvage. No further action is required. No forgiveness, no cleansing, no purification is required. You are whole as you are. You are blessed and perfect from the moment of conception, for all lives before this one. You are blessed from the time before time.

Is soul growth pleasant? It is not. All change requires movement. All transformation requires change. When you move a bone that has long been broken and has been set incorrectly, when you move that bone into a position where it can grow straight and heal, there is considerable discomfort and pain. But the result, a clean straight bone, healing properly at last, will be meritorious to you in the end.

## Exercise

Consider this Lesson as a new, clean setting of yourself. There is no confession or absolution. You are already purified in God. Yet we ask you to understand your position, in this aspect. Please write:

1. Who is your worst enemy?

2. Who do you hate the most?

3. Who do you feel uncomfortable around? Who makes you feel angry, unpleasant, panicked, or in pieces?

4. Who have you never forgiven?

Thank you for writing these. It is difficult to have a broken heart. Do not worry about these questions, or your answers. Do not consider anything. Simply write what you feel, and let it be.

Remember, all pain is a wave. It is a vibrational wave that washes over you. For this reason, all pain and suffering can be felt, but it does not last forever. You may consider the manner in which a wave in the ocean comes. They roll upon each other, one after another, breaking on the shore. Yet they keep coming. If you consider that pain is only a wave, a wave that comes, rolls back, comes again, recedes, you will understand that eventually, a wave recedes.

All suffering is pain. All pain is suffering. All things that make your heart hurt are suffering. At the same time, we ask that you consider bliss, happiness, ecstasy. This is a wave as well. It also is finite. It is changeable, it washes over you; it washes through you.

If you feel suffering, remember it is a wave.

If you feel bliss, enjoy it and do not be sad when it ends.

These two aspects, suffering and bliss, are the same waves. They both will end in time. They both will come again.

# What is your unique soul?

∽

## MIRIAM

IN THIS LESSON YOU WILL be asked to identify your unique soul.

Your people have been tribal people. But the time for this is fast becoming decayed. The protection of the tribe, the gain of the tribe, the striving of nation against nation, group against group, faction against faction.

The time for this is nearly done.

Yet even while we work to bring you the Light, there are disturbances, there is static in the channel that is caused by the new communication.

We ask that you consider your aspect in the infinite uniqueness of your world. To be all One, each must find his or her own way. You cannot find it carried on the back of another. Without your own thought, you have no thought. For this reason we say:

Cults are cult.

Religions are cult.

Churches are cult.

Corporations are cult.

Sporting teams are cult.

Groups of all kinds are cult.

Morality is cult.

Religions use the guise of the word of God to attract and subdue people. We say, come to God. But do so from your own mind, and your own aspect. Do not allow the illusion of church to control what you think.

Sheep in a field will follow a leader into a path of oncoming cars. We see this. A shepherd may lead a flock easily. But we say, do not be sheep. Consider your own aspect. The time of the flock is over. You are not here to be led. You are here to lead yourselves.

God does not punish, God does not sanctify, God does not bring guilt or shame, control or dictate, preach or moralize. God is All Light. Do not believe otherwise.

Companies also, those firms who have captured the great wealth of the nations—these are cult. This is the worship of commerce, power, the idea that the world needs to be developed, that material well-being is of importance. These companies cause great evil and great good, and they are not God.

Do not worship the companies or their items. Find God in your own prayer, your writing, your meditation, in your own aching heart reaching for what is True. The companies are a passing figment and an imaginary aspect. They will not be long on the earth. There is no place for them in the new way.

What is to come is apocalyptic only in that the old way is being destroyed. A great transformation of all people is swirling within the masses, and understanding will continue until it becomes clear. We have sent you, and many others, to bring this message.

Sporting teams are cult. They are tribal, feudal. They are violent, and allow man and woman to celebrate acts of war.

Celebrities are cult. No human should worship another.

Shopping is cult. Materialism is useless.

Pornography is cult. It is sexual energy wasted on what is not real.

We ask you to consider these.

# Exercise

We do not mind if you are affronted by these questions. We are setting your bones. You are very close to the first opening of the heart, which will come by the next Lesson.

Consider your unique soul. Part of a part of the All, but also unique. As a snowflake is unique, but a part of all snow falling.

1. What cults do you belong to? Remember that all groups are cults.

2. If you were not in these cults, who would you be?

3. We ask that you define yourself by category, such as mother, wife, worker, race, religion and so on.

4. Which of these categories are cults?

5. Which categories do you enjoy the most?

6. Which categories make your heart hurt?

7. Without these categories, who are you?

8. We ask again. Without these categories, who are you?

# What is dark requires clearing.

## CONSTANCE

EVERY NEGATIVE OR DISTURBING IMAGE you see enters into the cells. It is the same as a disease. The negative energy from TV, viewing screen, whatever you see that is unpleasant or distasteful to your great goodness attaches to the cells, invades them like dirt, germ, cancer.

We do not have the words for this, but you have the words. A clearing is necessary to keep you in a state that is pure and good.

The seeing and hearing of something is the same as doing it.

<hr />

There is no sin, in the way that you believe. There is only what is light and what is dark, and what is dark requires clearing.

Many of you who are more sensitive, or have been more damaged, have a clear understanding of the negative, the darker, dense energies. You understand intuitively to stay away.

The energies in themselves are neither good nor bad. They are merely energies that you, soul in human form, mind in body, experience. Yet because you are human, the darker energies are harder to navigate, just as it would be hard to walk through a river of mud. This is why you choose the light. You can move through it more quickly. When you choose dark energies, you weight yourself down. You cannot move forward. You become stuck and are submerged.

Just as you have colors—red, blue, yellow, purple, orange—so each energy has its own sensibility for you. Dark, light, suffering, bliss, earthy, ethereal. Most of you will not understand any of this, but a few of you will.

When you become ascended, as some of you are or will be, the colors are easily identified. Not as color, but as energy. Thus you begin to recognize the energy as you meet it. As you enter into a time/space with it.

We will come back to this idea, when you have learned more.

## Exercise

These questions seem simple but they are not.

1. Write of a time when you were violent. This is unpleasant. We ask that you do this, and you look at it. Write the darkness, and allow this writing to come to us as a Truth.

2. Write of a time when you experienced violence at the hand of another.

3. Write of a time when you have seen violence in person.

4. Write of a time you have seen violence as an image.

If it is your wish to discontinue violence, and to be released from this energy field, write this to us now. Call upon us, and ask for dark to be surrounded by our glowing light. There is no time when we will not come. There is no time when we will not be there instantly, like a breath of wind on your shoulder.

# Disconnection and connection.

⌁

## CONSTANCE

DO NOT CLUTTER YOUR MIND with what is distraction. By this we mean the attention you give to what is only temporary and does not affect you.

When you are obsessed with ideas in your mind, they do manifest. The thoughts of sadness lead to more sadness, and the thoughts of joy and beauty—the term you use is abundance. When you believe in one thing, you call upon the Divine to prepare this for you. There is nothing you cannot have. But there is much you will not want. So it is important to stay clear in the mind, for the mind is the place where you are most apt to become confused.

The heart will not lie to you, my dear ones, the heart will tell you everything. The body reveals all. But the mind can be distracted; the mind can even fool itself. We see this with so many of you, whose hearts are open and full, but who have come to allow their minds to believe what is not True.

What is not True? Electronica is not true. This is a way only of manipulating energies. The Internet, as an obsession and distraction is not True, but it is a tool for connection, and it is the sign of what is new.

What is new is people becoming the leaders rather than the leaders leading. This is the new way: the people will lead themselves.

187

A friendship, such as you have on electronica—this is not friendship. Surely you know this? It is merely a reaching out into the ether of the collective soul. The collective soul is now young and excited, inviting and expanding. This particular aspect is immature—newly discovered. Like a child with a new toy, you are robust and eager and cannot believe the possibilities of this new tool.

Understand the tool you use. Consider if it is or is not True.

Know that you create your reality with your actions. We say this again: you create your reality with your actions. What you dream is made possible or manifested. But manifestation takes place in the act of doing.

This is the piece many of you still do not understand.

The mind begins the journey. The feet continue the path. There is of course, no destination except for God. In the act of manifestation, and in the taking on of the journey, this becomes clear. The objects of desire—house, spouse, child, money, car, world power, domination, fame, fortune, health, physical attractiveness—all these common material things that you manifest within this idea of limitless abundance.

Yet when you do reach your goal, you see that the journey has been made through God. You have no needs. There is nothing that you can desire that will mean more to you than God. To rest in God is the only thing that is useful to you.

## Exercise

These questions are involving.

1. Write of your disconnection. By disconnection, we mean times when you called upon God but did not hear a response, or to feeling the comfort of the Divine. There is no shame in

disconnection. We are always here, but you may not always find that you can connect with us. Many of you may not be sure if you have connected at all. This is part of the soul growth, learning how to connect with us at all times.

2. Next, and this is a joyous exercise, please write of a time when you felt most connected to God. This can be of course connection to God in any form, for God is God is God in all places, all peoples, all electrons and cells and energies. There is no difference. To connect to God is to lock into the hum, and these are joyous times.

Record these both: the disconnection, and the connection.

*Dear God. I feel nervous about taking these words down because it seems strange and seems blasphemous, and does not agree with many people's religions.*

We bring these words to you because we know that you will take them down carefully. We already know that you have the tools of the listener. That you can bring these words to fruition in the ears of the people. The people are clogged in their beliefs and their distractions, and need to hear clear guidance. We will use who we can use. You are one. There are others. On this day, there are many who have been sent for this purpose. You are one.

*I did not think I would do this.*

The needs of our time are great. You were sent here for this reason. This path and the path of your music and your voice are conduits for us.

*I am afraid.*

There is nothing to be afraid of in this process, even though the ideas are new to you and the language is strange.

*I don't know where it comes from.*

It comes from us, and thus we will give these words to you to dissipate and distribute in the ways we will arrange. You do not have to concern yourself about their distribution; all this is taken care of. This project for you is of showing up and letting us use your gifts and your words, and in allowing yourself to be one who will be utilized.

*I am afraid people will think I am crazy.*

There is only God. There is only connection and being with the Divine. That is all there is. We surround you, your guides and angels, and we give you the words that need to be distributed.

*What are your names?*

My name is Constance. I am the one who will bring you the most instruction. There is also Miriam; she is here for your support and sustenance, and will help you keep your heart open to come to this place and receive these words. There is Another to come later, but not at this time. His might is great.

*And Hajam is not here?*

Hajam is for you, my dear daughter. He is your own guide, but he is not for these Lessons. He supports you eternally, as you are chosen to be with him.

*Will I see you?*

If you wish to see us, you may.

*I wish to see you.*

It will be done.

*Is there another Lesson (at this time)?*

Yes, there is one more. We cannot give too much at one time. If you become tired you cannot hear the words clearly.

*I try to hear the words exactly.*

We know this. This is why you are chosen for this scripture.

## LESSON SEVEN

# On distractions.

‑ᴏ‑

## CONSTANCE

THE PURITY OF THE BODY makes it easier for you to hear the spirit.

The distraction of electronica is pervasive in the culture. Yet another way in which we see you becoming deaf to the hum is by distractions of the body. By this we mean what is physical, such as drugs, alcohol, sex, excessive exercising, excessive involvement with illness. All of these are the same—an extreme involvement with the body that is distraction.

We see that most people in the culture who can use drugs are using drugs. Drugs are herbs, drugs are medical, drugs are illegal drugs, doctor-prescribed drugs. Drugs are food, drugs are alcohol, drugs are drugs. When you take drugs, you lose yourself in an altered state, so you are not within your own reality. In this way, you cannot find your spirit easily.

This is one way you discover yourself disconnected from God.

We say this also for sex. Sex is a part of your earth body, and the act of sex may be a sacred act. But sex taken as a drug, as distraction, as a way of blocking what you feel, so you do not feel the real bliss of spirit. This is another matter.

We ourselves are not sexual beings; this has become a process from which we have been lifted. We do not require sex for our needs, just as we do not require the other elements of the earthly body.

Of the earthly body, we must clarify to you, because there are other bodies which are not of earth, an infinite number, surely you know this by now and will come to know it.

The universe is limitless. There are others, many other physical bodies, and they are also One of the One, in the same way that you are.

⟨◇⟩

Food is also distraction. The idea of filling yourself up with food so that you have excess abundance with food.

Alcoholism, what you call an addiction, is another method of changing the state of mind.

Illness, this is also a distraction. Your body is perfect and perfectly constructed. There is nothing you cannot wish for yourself that your body cannot obtain.

Pain is also distraction.

These distractions—you do not have to choose them. They assuage the feelings of heartbreak, fear, sadness, grief; they assuage the feelings of shame, and regret. But these are not required.

Again we say: these distractions are not required.

Consider a man who can easily walk on his own feet, but who discovers that he has a thorn in his toe. He begins to use a crutch. After a while the thorn is dissolved into his skin, and the pain is gone. But he continues to use the crutch. So too do you use your addictions, your binges, your illness, your overeating, your sexual excesses, your indulgence.

These are not required by you. You can walk as you are, without these.

As your understanding becomes more clear and you can see and hear the spirit more closely guiding you, these elements will drop away.

They are not required by you.

What is required is the Divine. The physical is a mirage.

## Exercise

Write to us of your distractions, in these areas of the physical realm, and tell us of your shame and discomfort. Then, if you would like, ask for help from us. We are of the angelic realm, and all that you ask is yours.

# The state of dis-ease.

## CONSTANCE

So, YOU HAVE RETURNED AGAIN, after all your fears?

*Yes.*

This is good. There are no fears. Let us begin.

Consider the word you have given disease. Dis-ease. A lack of ease within you. A constant fear of what you are.

There is no fear.

There are many elements on earth right now that contribute to this dis-ease, to this depression, to this lack of energetic force.

The first stems from the innate toxicity of your environment. You know that the trees, the waters, the airs, all the clearing forces, cannot work efficiently with the contaminants that are in the world's ether. They cannot do their job of breathing in dirty, breathing out clean, of the proper exchange of water, of dissipation and dissolution. They cannot do this.

All is related together. Nature is a strong force, one of the most healing forces you have on your planet. Without nature, you are a lost people.

The toxicity that comes from overconsumption of goods, this is a problem you have to manage. If you do not manage it, your people will get sicker and sicker.

The problems of the seeping toxicity, by these we mean the drugs, the other pharmacologies that have appeared in the waters, in the streams.

These affect you no end.

My children. You must understand that this is not the way.

The first depression comes from being in a setting that is seeping with poisons. You must find your own space to be cleared. You must clear the earth and allow the exchanges to clear, and to begin again a state of efficiencies.

The second depression comes from not doing what you are meant to do.

In this country, there are many jobs that are unfit for the lowest life forms of creation, and we see that all life is sacrificed here. They are the life of the wretch.

Without a job that feeds your soul, my child, there is no point in working at all. The harm that is caused by taking on an occupation that is not true to you, that you are not true to, cannot be measured.

This life on earth is your possibility for soul growth; that is the goal. This life is for your experience of beauty, joy, love, companion-ship, nature, God, God, God.

Thus, the hours that you spend in each day, for you count them as such, are of utmost importance.

For this question, we ask that you consider your current work, that is, the way in which you spend your time.

# Exercise

1. What is it that you do on this earth, with your hour time?

2. What is it that you would prefer to do?

We do not ask you to make the changes. We ask only that you describe what is in your heart. If you do not know in your heart, we ask you to answer this question, after a brief period of meditation:

3. What is in your heart?

If you still do not know what is in your heart, we ask you to breathe deeply, close your eyes, and ask the angels to come to you. When you feel they have surrounded you, ask the angels for their guidance.

# Purity of the body.

～

## CONSTANCE

A TREE REQUIRES AIR, SOIL, water. It remains rooted, it sees all, it sways in wind and weather. This creation grows from a tiny pod into a towering being, a being that may live as long or longer than you.

It requires no shelter, nothing more than what surrounds it, to live.

You are not a tree. But your requirements are the same. Your body, your human body is a gift. It is perfectly and reverently balanced. It is filled with all you need to live, the inflow, the outflow, the blood, the circulation, the many functions of your human body. And yet what you provide to it is not enough.

You would not breathe dirt for air?

You would not drink stone for water?

These things cannot sustain.

Thus, the foods you eat, that which you imbibe, these things must be clean. They must be as simple as the water for the tree.

What has become on the earth is a place that is overpowered by medications, hormones, drugs, alcohol, additives, flavorings, chemicals pollutant, toxic.

This is shame to your body. It is unusable. It is of danger to you.

You would not drink stone for water?

And yet you drink cans of chemical.

You would not eat dirt for food?

And yet you pour packets of chemical, you heat food in packets.

This cannot be. There comes a time when balance is out of balance, when balance is no longer possible in the body; this is when you get sick.

You get sick from the heart being out of balance, from the heart holding too much pain. The heart absorbs and dissipates pain like a song, but after a point, there is too much pain, and the pain attacks the body.

This is so simple, my dear ones. Surely this is known to you?

The heart must be cleared, continually and always, by revealing and gifting of your heart to us, by allowing us to take your burdens and your pains, and giving this to us.

Your body must be kept clear in the earthly manner. When you plea for healing, you must also make it easy for us to send the energy to you, by keeping your body free from chemicals and damaging substances.

The more clear you are, the more we can send energy to you. The more clear you are, the more you can receive the light and the love which is sent.

We are always here. But the other substances, they act as deadening for your body. The life force is in everything you eat. Drink. Breathe. The more pure you can be, the more clear, the more we can bring the energy to you, the more you can connect, the better you can hear us, the more you will know peace.

Take the gravel out of your body, your heart, your ears.

Take the stone out of your cup.

Drink water that is clean, that nourishes and that quenches the thirst.

Eat food that is healing.

Take the rocks out of your ears.

## Exercise

If you desire to become clear, if you desire to bring your body to a new state, please write that you would like us to help you.

# Writing as prayer.

꙰

## CONSTANCE

WE HEAR THE PRAYERS FROM you; there is no time on this earth when a prayer is not being said, mumbled, cried out, whispered.

In your journal, we ask that you write your prayers to us.

We do not want your prayers to be of a flowery, forced nature, or a recitation of what others have said, or that you have read, or been prescribed.

We want to hear your prayers as cries for help, for guidance, for assistance, of gratitude, of confusion, of pain, of suffering. We want to hear your cries, written by you.

In the act of writing, there is an act of transformation.

## Exercise

1. What are your dreams?

2. What do you need help with?

3. What sorrows, shames, and worries would you like to be lifted?

4. Would you like to see God?

5. Would you like signs that we have heard you?

# The answering of prayers.

༄

## CONSTANCE

THE PRAYERS OF AND MUMBLINGS of earth are infinite; they are un-ending and unstoppable, as has been through all times. And yet the prayers of the universe are also infinite, with more worlds than you can imagine.

⊸◇⊸

*I can't hear you.*
Take a breath.
*It is hard to hear. Are we done?*
No, take a breath.

⊸◇⊸

Prayers are answered in the timing of God. God does not answer in the timing of earth. God answers in the timing of the soul's growth. You will hear when you are ready to hear. You cannot hear before you can hear. When you pray through voice or writing or all the ways you pray, we come to you instantly. We surround you with Divine bliss. This is constant. There is no exception.

This is intense for you. We will close this session very soon.

Those who do not know Jesus are missing the point. Those who deny Buddha or any of the saints or prophets—it is the same. All

Holy Beings are One with the One. All Holy Beings are methods and ways and examples for which you may emulate how they have lived, what they have taught, and what they have done.

They are sent to remind you.

They are sent to open your eyes.

If you do not know how to act, act like Jesus. If you do not know how to be, be like the Dalai Lama, always laughing in the midst of great trial. If you do not know how to be, be as Mother Theresa, taking the poorest of the poor to her body, feeding them, cleaning them, praying with them.

If you cannot do this, then do what you can.

Sri Amma and all the saints spread joy. Jesus spoke and taught with the illuminated word of God; follow His word. Follow the word of all Holy Beings. There is a list of saints and prophets and Holy Beings that is never-ending.

And look also at the Holy Ones all around you. You are all holy, but there are some of you, in this very day, who shine with the light of God. It burns from their skin. Consider these people. Surround yourself with them. Be like them, with illuminated skin.

We do not file on morality; this is for you to discover. When you begin to act with the acts of the Holy Ones, you become holy, and the practices that are of depravity, sickness, cruelty—these will drop off like false layers of skin; you will be only left in your new, bare skin, free in the spirit.

## Exercise

1. Please write down the names of ten saints. By saints we mean all Holy Beings. These may also be saints who are found in your daily life.

2. Please say a blessing for each.

# Opening of windows.

## CONSTANCE

THERE ARE WAYS THAT YOU are love, with love, in only the state of love.

There are ways that you are not in the state of love.

You may choose.

We send signs and symbols to you at all times. Many of you find it easy to understand our voices. Others cannot hear or see at this time. The way we communicate with you is endless, but because of the separation of our realities, it can be difficult for you to see and hear us. We are in all of all time, whereas most of you are not of all time yet. By this we mean cognizance. This will come to you later, in other lives and as you grow.

You are not very old. Some of you are ancient, but many of you are not very old. There is much to be learned.

We ask that you consider the way of the universe, of the earth's connection to our realm. This is no place. There is no time. We are what we are. We are all perfect, and all inclusive, and all One. But you prefer, sometimes, to see us as above, in heaven or another place. It is of no matter or difference to us.

One way for you to consider us is to imagine an orange, wrapped in-side another orange, inside another, inside yet another. Now imagine that within the skin of one of the layers of this infinitely wrapped orange, there is a hole—a window or point of conduit.

And also, on the next layer that is beneath or above, there is also this same hole, window, or point of conduit. This is the same for all the layers, inside and outside each other.

Now, take one layer and twist it so that its window is aligned with the window of the next layer—either inner or outer. Here at this point, there is connection—a conduit or channel.

It is even possible for us, but not for you, to twist each layer of the orange around, so that all windows, in each layer, are opened to each other. At this point there is pure conductivity between the innermost and the outermost.

Of course there are infinite layers to this orange, which is as small as you might imagine, or as large. Of course they would conduct infinitely.

So is it with the realms, with time, with space.

This is one way we reach you. We find a place where there is a window or an opening through some person or community, and we open our window so there is connection between both.

We are not able to connect with you, when your window is not open.

We ask that you please open all your windows! We have much to tell you!

For some, your window is mostly open—for others it is firmly closed. With beings of bliss and transcendence, the window is open all the way at all times. This is the case for the Holy Ones. In infants, and in many animals; certainly in the trees.

## Exercise

Please write for us now what you believe is your path to God. By this we mean not your soul work, which is always occurring. We mean your earth work.

1. In what earth work are you on your path to God?

If this question is too difficult, please answer in the more common way:

2. What purpose do you have here?
3. What is the path that will give you bliss and connection?

There is no interpreter required for you, no guru, no priest or psychic. Take the direct path. The window may be opened on your side by you, and when the window is open, we are able to converse with you clearly and easily.

# LESSON THIRTEEN

# Chaos and peace.

◦

## CONSTANCE

THE CONFUSION THAT YOU FIND yourself in is not unusual. When you transcend what is chaos, you attain a state of peace.

To some of you, the idea of peace is idly dull, boring. How could this not be to you, when you are so often immersed in the electronica, in the media, in the traffic and the roar?

We say, beware of these forces. They are often in the state of machine that came to you, in the times of exploration and conquering, of machine industry and the new mega-commerce. With all new forces, there are those who maraud, pillage, rape, steal; there are those who conquer. This is happening even now in this world, even when you do not see it. There are ways of marauding where the forces are kept more hidden, and they involve you without announcing their presence beforehand.

Do you notice now the prevalence of the TV screen, or the computer screen in so many places? All this creates a type of group thought, not a thought that emerges from the group, as a collective consciousness, but a collective sham. It is beneath you, and who you are. Sports, TV shows, comedies, sex, pornography, religious, shopping channels, the drama shows, the reality shows, nearly everything; the other shows that will come even as the media becomes more and more desperate for the sale of their goods and services.

These are the gladiator blood sport of ancient times, these are the bullfights, these are the slaughter of each other. They bring you feelings of disgust, enrapture, of interest and excitement, a shameful feeling that is not fear. With these you lose your sensitivity. When you see this way, when others watch with the greatest interest, you think it is important.

It is not important.

It is all falseness. It is fantasy, it is non-reality, it is an enormous mirage, it contains no sustenance.

Neither is there air in it for you to breathe, nor water for you to drink. There is no manna in this for you.

What is real is God.

When you finally begin to understand that it is only in God's delight that you can be happy, in the way that you understand happy: a freedom of anxiety, a freedom of conflict, a freedom from stress.

To reach this state you must go where God is, which is not in the electronica.

To be real is to see God.

To lie on a beach, with the sand under your body, and to have your mind unclouded by waves in the electronica. This is the way.

To sit in your human skin.

To sit in your spirit skin.

Many of you have lost your sensitivity, and this makes it more difficult to understand.

It is not about right and wrong. It is about being with or being away from God.

If your sensitivities are dulled, it is hard to believe.

But we ask you this: can you believe in this a little?

You know the sensations of shame, of overindulgence, of bloating of the mind and spirit. It is the damage that comes from this accord—from your absence from God. For remember: God is never absent from you; it is only you who are absent from God.

The other planets, and there are countless numbers, also affect you, but it is not time for you to understand this. You will know of this in the future; some of you will be living in your same bodies, when this time comes.

For even as you are all One of One, this is not limited to the earth planet on which you find yourself. The earth planet is one of many where the Ones are. You are One with the Ones not of earth, as well as with the Ones of earth.

This idea may be difficult for you.

In that place where you have met prejudice and failed, and have had no tolerance for difference, this idea—that the Ones who are from other places are also One of One—may be difficult for you. It is only with great love and with God that this will not be a struggle.

The color of skin will be less important, the difference of language and culture will be less of a difference when you are all under the banner of Earth. But when the other is from other, some of you will struggle. Some of you will be in awe.

This is not the time for this yet, but it will be soon enough for some of you to see this. Be ready, and hold God with an open heart.

The universe is: all One, all expanding, without division or separation.

## Exercise

1. Please explain how you feel when you are watching TV, a movie, using the Internet. Tell us about the exhilaration, the need, the feeling of being flat when the electronica is removed.

2. What does it feel like to you to sit quietly, with bare hands? How long can you sit this way, in your human skin? Do you become anxious?

3. What is it like for you to go into a store that is filled with items to buy—beautiful, colorful items, and to look with eyes only and to buy nothing?

4. What is it like for you to give away 20 percent of your possessions? 40 percent?

5. If you had to leave your home today, what are the things that you would bring with you? What objects would you most require to bring with you?

6. Consider, today, stepping out into the world without money, credit cards, cell phone, identification. With nothing that defines you as subset, nothing that defines you except as human being.

7. Consider if you are enough.

You are enough. As you are, at this moment. We bring you this, so that you can understand it. Even if you are separate from God at this moment, in a blink of an eye, you may become One with the One. There is no separation, except for what you choose.

Ask, if you wish, to become whole with God.

It is done upon asking.

# The need to listen.

## CONSTANCE

AM I DOING THE RIGHT *thing?*

(Laughter.) There is no need to even ask this question, Beloved. You know this. We are giddy with excitement and euphoria. This is what we have placed into works, and there are no worries. We will tell you entirely what to say.

*I may be embarrassed.*

This feeling is a feeling that you are getting over quickly, and will have no place for you.

*I am confused about spirit guides.*

Spirit guides are those who have been chosen for you. Hajam is the spirit guide of you; he will be with you until that time when you pass into your next realm. Right now you are speaking with Constance, who is not a spirit guide or a guardian angel, but of the angelic realm. She is working with you for these logos that are required to go into the world.

There are people waiting to read this book who are in desperate need of this information, and this is why Constance gives you this information quickly, so that the information may be dissipated in the most efficacious fashion. Miriam is another guide in this book, and she will be helping in different ways. And as we have told you, there is Another to come.

*What will this book be?*

It will be an instruction. It will be a disclosure of your own experience. And there will be these Lessons, 33 of them. You will also teach these teachings to others, so they will know how to do this. You will also share some of your private secrets, which will be difficult for you, but will add to the humanity of what is.

Not everyone listens in prayer. They pray for what they want, but they do not wait for the answer. What we teach you is about listening for the Divine answer.

Many people have forgotten to listen, only to ask.

Sometimes it seems to us that everyone is shouting requests, when what is required is to listen—to be patient and to silken, like a small pool of water that only occasionally has a ripple of wind. When such water receives the wind, it knows. From stillness, the entire pool can begin to feel this ripple.

When you are a wave machine, you cannot feel the wind.

You must listen, daughter, and by you we mean you, and we also mean all of the others.

For this Lesson, we ask that you understand the need to listen. We ask that you put down your goals of manifestation, because while the universe will answer any prayer you have, it is not always in the best interest of your Divine soul. Your soul knows what you need, but your human self does not. It is not that your human self is more base or lower. It is just living within a different realm, a different time/space illusion, and it is more liable to distraction.

When you speak with God, it is not simply a matter of shouting for help, or shouting for more money, or the material things you want. It is not a matter of shouting out what you want: "Oh please God, please God." It is two-way connection. When you pray, or meditate, or when you channel God into writing, it is a Direct Path. You communicate with God. God communicates back to you.

But do you listen, my sons and daughters?

⋘◇⋙

Your heart speaks to you in God's words. Your heart is the most easily understood tool that you can use. Your heart, your body tells you what you feel. When you feel happy, comfortable, safe, loved. Then, my dearest ones, you are in the right place. But when you feel uncomfortable, abused, addicted, unsettled, unhappy, miserable, depressed. Then you are not in the right situation.

If you are in places where you cannot feel loved, comfortable, pleased with yourself, you are not with God. How unhappy it is, to be separated from God!

## Exercise

1. We ask you again, what is your life path? If you do not know, please ask us to tell you.

2. What is the next precise, perfect step that you can take? If you do not know, please ask us to tell you.

Again, my children, we ask only for you to write what is the next step. When you hear the answer, do not question it or discount it, or tell yourself it is not important. We ask only that you write it. For example, if you see a guitar in the window of a shop, and you are told that you should buy the guitar, but you do not know how to play guitar—this is being told what is the next step.

You do not have to know why.

You do not have to know how.

You do not need to understand—you may even understand that you cannot understand at this time.

# Your heart is what holds you on earth.

⟿

## CONSTANCE

My children, it is important to listen to your heart. Your heart is the way in which you know how you feel. This is one of the ways that we reach you.

When your heart is sad, you may turn to us for comfort. Simply turn inward for a moment, take the inhale and the exhale, and request us. A rush of wings and we have arrived. We have surrounded you with our presence and our healing.

When we have come near, when you feel us as a lightness behind your eyes, as a flutter at your shoulder, as a warmth that spreads inside your bodies where you might have felt cold before.

Bring us all your wants and needs, all your fears and sorrows; bring us your whole heart, my darlings. Bring us your whole heart, which is all that is in it. We know your heart already, but bring it to us as a gift, as your offering.

For your heart is what holds you on earth; it is not your soul. Your soul is limitless and free, and it is one of the One.

◈

Your heart is what holds you on earth.

By heart, we mean both the physical heart, the beating, circulating of blood that keeps you alive, but also your spiritual heart—all of

212

your longing, dreams, illusion, rage, sorrow, compassion, tenderness, hatred. You are all of this.

When you give us your heart, we hold it gently. Are we not the same? One is always One. There is no distinction.

Your heart comes to us, and we know it clearly. Thus we say: give them all to us, your fears, your strengths, your cares and worries, all of it. And let us make use of them for the world.

Let us make use of all of you.

If you choose to give yourself to us, to the One, to God, the Divine, to Yahweh, Buddha, Jesus, all the names you have for what is One, then you allow your heart to be given freely—your earth heart.

And you will hear what we hear, your eyes will shine with God's light, and your ears will resound with the sound of music and trumpets, the call of angelic.

This is such glory. Such glory to God.

And your heart will be healed, your body will be healed, your whole body will be ablaze with light and fire and brim with goodness.

Such is what happens when you are transformed in light.

## Exercise

1. What would it take to give your heart to that which is Divine, the one of One? Let tears come—they cleanse and fall like a cleansing rain.

2. What is required for you to be healed?

3. After you have written what you require to be healed, please request from us the healing.

The moment you have thought the words, the moment you have asked in your mind and in your writing, it is done.

My child, it is done before you have asked.

# Manifesting from the heart.

## CONSTANCE

WE WILL RETURN TO THE idea of manifesting. This is a new idea that has become known to you, and it is a correction.

In manifesting, you ask for what you believe you want. You ask for what you believe you want, when in reality, you require nothing.

You require nothing for your soul. You require nothing for your Being, which is perfect. What your heart longs for cannot be satisfied by material things, by promotions, the nicer car, the new lover.

What the heart longs for is peace.

Thus, when you manifest, when you ask for what you say your heart desires, please remember what your heart does not require.

We will bring you what you ask for. But it is more useful to know what you will really be pleased with, than to ask for things that will only make you more filled with longing, miserable with desire, still with a bruised and hurt heart.

What the heart longs for is peace. What the heart longs for is connection. Connection to God. Connection to other, of all the collective soul, the collective heart.

The connection to the ephemeral is real; that of nature, the wind, the water, all that is and surrounds you. The connection to the spiritual realm, the other worlds, times and spaces and planes—this is also real.

It is these things that will satisfy you.

The other things are not worth asking for.

You will receive them, but like a child with too many toys, they will fall on the floor unused, broken, discarded.

If you ask for what you do not require, you will receive it.

Far better it is, my children, to you and you and you who are practicing manifesting, to ask for peace in your heart. To pray and meditate and ask for peace in your heart.

Thus instead of manifesting, of creating, of using the I, the ego to create and attract and swirl and stir up, you may use these same forces to bring peace, enlightenment, love to all Beings.

This is true manifestation. The transformation of all into the eternal, infinite Now.

## Exercise

1. We ask that you make a list of what your earth heart would desire: the car, the money. Write everything down that you would desire, listing everything that could possibly make you happy. Write thirty things, if you can think of that many. Now, take this list and put it in a place you will look at it again, in three months time.

Do not ask for anything now, my child. Put the list away; do not ask, and do not look at it until three months have passed. Put the list away, without asking, without acting, without manifesting.

Then wait, my dear ones.

2. Now, please write these words: *Dear God. Please tell what is of the highest good for me to manifest. Please let me know this answer now.*

# Your earth heart is your greatest tool.

## CONSTANCE, GABRIEL

WE WISH FOR YOU TO be happy, dear ones.

What will make your earth heart whole?

A new guide comes to speak to you, and he is of the highest call-ing. He is mighty, Archangel Gabriel. Yet he arrives without fire or blaze of glory. He is a new voice. He arrives to the Lesson, and he will provide you with more.

God's glory is upon is. It is the most tender love of all.

There is much to be sorrowful in your world. Yet in the face of the greatest tragedies and sorrows, there exists also the same notion of the earth heart.

The earth heart feels. It is your greatest tool.

Yet many of you have encased your hearts, your heart's heart, into boxes of tin, boxes of cement and stone; stone heart, closed heart.

The true heart is tender, compassionate. The sacred heart is tender.

To feel compassion is to hold sadness inside, and to allow it to dis-sipate through you, into the world.

The eternal knows no sadness. You are eternal, and you are Now, but you are also human, with an earth heart.

Your earth heart is designed to break a million times. It is designed to break and cleave asunder; it is created to hold the most compassion, the most fear and doubt and tenderness, the most sorrow.

It is designed for you to feel fully and completely, and to feel beyond yourself.

It is designed for you to live with the open heart of pain, the open heart of fear, all open to all feelings, the greatest joys, the greatest sufferings.

Again, we say: the purpose of the human heart is to hold that feeling, and to understand what it is to be of the world.

This is your life on the earth.

## Exercise

The soul continues.

But the earth heart holds what it knows. It beats of pain, shame, suffering, the screaming cry in the wilderness, the agony of fear, the great discontent. This is your heaving, human heart.

Tell us again, today, what is in your heart.

Please write to us of your heart.

What you did not tell us before, please tell us now.

Write your heart to us in all its turmoil.

And when you are done, recognize that your heart is healed.

Question your angels, question your spirit guides, all the Holy Ones. Question all of those with answers! You have come before us as One in the family of the human heart, in the heart's meticulous misery. Request from us the healing of your heart, the peace of your heart, the assuage and grace of your heart.

Even as you write these words, the healing is arrived to you.

# LESSON EIGHTEEN

# Your heart is a vessel for compassion.

⟡

## CONSTANCE

THE PURPOSE OF HAVING AN earth heart is to use it as a vessel for compassion. The heart is the place where you may contain all your pain, and also all your joy.

You speak of heavy heart, heart broken or small heart or big heart. Your heart is a vessel for your emotional energy; we ask that you consider what emotions you allow yourself to feel fully.

You also speak of open heart, clean heart.

But we seek a heart that feels not just for self, but for the other.

I is nothing.

You are nothing.

I is One.

You are One.

We are One.

One is One.

There is no separation between self and other.

To feel this in your heart, it is required that you take on the compassion for another. When you look at the face of the other, do not be tricked by the glittering ornamentation. Many people of earth have different ornamentation, but all is affect and stimulation. It is not incorrect to ornament, decorate, paint, and captivate attention to your body—your life is physical; it is an earth life as well as a spiritual life.

But we ask that you see beyond. That you hold the attractant, the irritant, the stimulant in one part of your gaze, and with your heart's eye, look to the heart of another.

We do not ask you look at the soul. The soul, your soul and another's soul—a soul is already perfect.

But a heart is for holding compassion.

Look for another, and understand this: their pain, their feeling, their fear, their anger, all is no more or less than yours.

## Exercise

We ask you now to examine the contents of your heart as you might imagine the treasures in a small box.

1. What are treasures that you store? List the treasures of your heart.

2. Now, choose a person you know or do not know. It is not important which you choose. Please imagine the contents of their heart, the treasures that they store. The memories, the joy, the tenderness. We ask you to list the treasures that another stores.

All hearts are brimming with all emotion.

In the compassion of your heart, is there room for another? How many can you add to your own heart?

Close your eyes now, and breathe in fully to the belly, breathe out to exhale. Imagine your heart expanding and widening, as you invite those you know in: the friend, the child, the spouse, the partner, the lover, the father, the mother, the sister, the brother, the other, the other, the other, the enemy. Invite as many as you can hold. Picture your chest expanding, a flap opening in your physical body, yourself tucking the other inside your physical body effortlessly, easily, without pain, each disappearing into the next.

When you think there are no more that you can hold, please add more.

When you can hold no more, please invite God, Jesus, Mohammed, Sri Amma, all the great saints, mystical beings, and Holy Ones, please ask them in also.

When you have asked these Holy Beings, please also ask all the angels and spirit guides.

When you have done this, and your heart is brimming with love, please ask yourself to come into your own heart.

Make room. Make room for the self that is All One.

# LESSON NINETEEN

# On releasing anger.

<p>

## MIRIAM

My dear ones. I come from a time and place where marriage was a life cast. If you married fortunately, your life might be enjoyable. If the match was not good, it was a disaster for all parties, not only the two involved, but also the children, the family, the entire community.

In this day you are divorcing. We say, there is more to the match than simply finding another attractive. Sex, lust, attraction, all these things belong to your species. But you must know your heart. And you must know your spirit selves—not only whom your earth heart longs for.

Your earth heart longs for many. But there will be only a few, or one, or none, who will fill your spirit. This one who fills your spirit is your Beloved, your true love. You have this understanding from your books, and your literature; it has been written so through the ancients.

My children, there is no point in being with another who is not your True One.

To be with a person who does not fill your spirit is just a passing of time; you would be better served by being alone.

The natural, balanced state of your earth body has two states: peace and bliss. But most of you do not feel these states. The earth body is clogged and poisoned.

The way to release the poison is to pray, or to contact us. You may contact us at any time; surely you know this? You may contact us when you are rising, when you are talking, when you are making a meal or working, and always, when you are in nature.

We ask that you let your hearts be cleansed from the pain of divorce, of separation, of the poison that you have allowed to be exchanged between you and other. For poison cannot be given without its agreement to be received. It is an exchange between two entities. Such is the way of the energies of earth and of Divine Law.

## Exercise

Take the deep breath in the nose, fill the belly, exhale out the nose a few times, and close your eyes.

Imagine your enemy as a tiny baby, and you as its mother or father. Hold this tiny baby in your arms, and watch as it sleeps peacefully.

We are all each other's children. We are all each other's parents. We are all mother, father, guardian, sister, infant to each other.

Now imagine you are holding this child's parent, their mother or father, deeply and gently in your arms, and rocking it, rocking it sweetly. Stare down at this new baby.

Now imagine you are holding this new child's parents, your enemy's father's father as a baby; your enemy's mother's mother. This new baby is the sweetest baby. You are rocking, rocking. You would provide this baby with all.

Now imagine you are holding yourself in your own arms, as a baby. Send loving kindness to yourself.

Hold all these babies, one after another, and send them the sweetest, most golden love, and ask for the end to receiving poison, and the end to giving poison. Think only of the golden orb of energy that extends between you and these babies.

When you are finished, bless them and release them, and return to your self. When you have opened your eyes, please write upon these questions.

1. In what way may I continue to release my anger and poison toward the person in question?

2. In what way may I continue to protect myself from future poison from this person?

Consider this idea, as you come into connection with this person, or think about this person in your daily life.

## LESSON TWENTY

# Everything is contained in spirit.

⌐

## CONSTANCE

ALL WAYS ARE AVAILABLE TO you, my child. It is only for you to decide what you wish. We ask that you consider that your earth heart is your tool in guiding you to where the spirit leads.

There is no life except in the spirit. Even your earth heart, with all its confusion of emotions and sorrows and extremes, knows this.

There is no place to go.

There is no place to see.

Everything is contained in spirit, and you may learn this quickly or slowly.

It does not matter at the speed of which you learn; it only matters that you do learn.

If you do not learn you are sent back to the beginning again. Look at the board games you have played—when you are sent back to "Go." We find these amusing. These games teach life. Your earth life and also the life of the spirit, in which you must certainly go back and start again on the path, almost as if from the beginning.

By continually being as the beginner—there is no shame in this. By continually beginning at the beginning, you become closer to spirit.

And yet. Spirit is available to you in the instant you seek it; surely this is clear to you? All you need do is to close your eyes, breathe in, breathe out, and spirit is with you, you are in spirit. This is the secret of finding spirit in your earth body.

## Exercise

Today, we seek to know your heart. We wish to know what you desire the most. We wish that you place this in writing. Both methods, the mind and writing are effective, but writing brings things forward and to fruition quickly.

1. Who do you believe you are? Please write this in detail.
2. Who would you prefer to be? Please write this in detail.

# Time has no meaning in spirit.

## CONSTANCE

WE COME TO YOU AS you believe.

In this we mean we come to Jesus as Jesus. We come to Buddha as Buddha. We come to those with other names as spirit guides. We come to you in as many names as there are.

We provide personality; this one who imparts this information—this one is Constance. She is a One. We come to you, the scribe. But for the others, the scribes who will come later—they will not hear this same Constance.

Constance is for this purpose only.

The other One, Miriam, is for another purpose.

The One Gabriel, who is brighter and more beautiful still, arrives in a cloud of golden light.

We ask that you close your eyes and do the breath of spirit suspension. In this breath we ask that you receive the presence of whoever will appear to you, and you ask the spirit for the name it is called. If it is Jesus, this will be so. If it is another angel or guide, this will be so. If there is no thing—if it is Holy Spirit or source or cosmos, this is what it is. There is no correct way to receive spirit.

All ways are correct.

We ask that you consider time—time passes quickly, or slowly, or not at all, as you have been taught to believe. Time can be measured, you say.

But we say: there is no time.

Time is infinity; it stretches all ways. No piece or slice can be measured. It is all infinite.

Space is infinite mass.

Time is also infinite.

We ask you to consider time as infinite bands or strips, horizontally. Time is one band placed or stacked upon the next, flowing forward or back. Each band stacked atop the next, forever. Within one band, there is you. Above you is another band. Below you, another band. Infinitely.

Yet there are no minutes. There are no seconds. All is Now, interconnected, live. One slice is the same as ten thousand years.

This is hard for you to understand, but if you allow this into your knowledge even if you cannot understand it, you will soon see that the mind can transcend time easily and without folly. Some of you may be able to learn this.

Thus your death, which is merely the death of your earth body and not of your soul, is of no importance to you. It is of significance, but it does not matter. How could it be, that your soul can end? Your soul is infinite, it is One of One.

Your earth body returns to earth: plant and air and earth again. It is the humus of the natural order. But the spirit body is eternal and effortless, it is light and rapture, and there is no end.

Time has no meaning in spirit.

Consider now, earth time, for your earth body, and how sick it has made you, and the anxiety that is brought on by it.

We are here, and we understand with compassion that this is not easy for you. It is beyond some minds; only to some will it be clear.

## Exercise

Consider your time, your minutes and seconds. Consider them now.

1. Write your time—your schedule for this day. Write this in detail.

2. Write your day as you might prefer it.

Time is sleight of hand, it is juggling, it is illusion. One second lasts ten thousand years in spirit. It is the earth body that is confused. Consider on earth, how you would prefer to inhabit your time.

# Communicating without electronica.

CONSTANCE

YOU ARE LEARNING THE WAYS of being connected through electronica. This is a method of using energy—of using energy vibrations to connect from one soul to another. You do this now with technology. But there will come a time when technology is no longer required.

This has become clear to many of you already.

Especially those who are young, who are learning to use this electronica in their earth bodies—after a while, your energy transfer will become automatic. Your souls will communicate without electronica.

Souls can do this now, at any time, and some of you do this already. But the energy transfer through electronica—it is the template for how you will learn. We see the energy of electronica as it transmits images and sound—these are methods of connecting energies across the world.

Your soul can do this without the middle step of technology.

By this we mean it is already possible in your earth body.

Try this now. Hold in your mind the image of a person with whom you wish to connect. Think thoughts of loving kindness to this person. Hold their face in your hands; in your mind look deeply into their eyes. Do this for one person, then another, then another. Connect deeply to the other's soul. This might be your child, lover, friend. It might be a person that you have not seen for a long time or who lives very far away. Study with loving kindness the face that you hold in your mind.

Now, when you are done, write the message that has come from each person down, and also write a message you would like them to know. Do not mention this message to the other.

Simply wait.

You will see results that are transformative to you and this person.

In the times of past, the idea of praying for another was a method of connection in this same way. But your minds are changing and growing very quickly, so there will be new ways of connection.

Again we say: already for some this is the way it is happening.

Most of you have this ability. Only a very few will be resistant when the time comes to make this change.

You will also be able to connect with those who have gone before you. At this time, the Others initiate contact with you; most of you are not able to initiate contact in the same way with them. Only a very few, a small group of you, are able to pull back this veil and go into this direction as initiates.

Yet in the time of many of your lives, this will become possible—to connect deeply with the soul spirit of those who have gone before.

We tell you this even though it will make many of you feel confused or distressed. Remember, earth body, earth mind—all is illusion. To work with illusion, you must understand all is One, all is connected, all is complete and whole in God. There is nothing that is not possible with God; that you can conceive of, or that you cannot even begin to bring into the framework of your mind.

## Exercise

1. Please write down the name of a loved one who has gone before you, and send thoughts of loving kindness to this person.

2. Please notice when you receive signs from this person.

# LESSON TWENTY-THREE

# Suffering and bliss are the same.

⌐ⴰ

## CONSTANCE

THIS WORLD, THE EARTH WORLD, is a harsh place at this time. All is interconnection; yet it is difficult for those souls who are more sensitive, or who are growing very fast, to comprehend the violence, the ugliness, the shame and horror that are a part of your earth world.

There is nothing to be done for this but to send out more love.

This is difficult for all souls, but especially for those souls who wish to hide away from the stronger, darker energies. In this we do not mean evil; we mean simply the energy that is more forceful in its expression.

There is suffering in the world, and there are those who choose the path of suffering.

There is bliss in this world, and there are a smaller number of you who choose the path of bliss.

It is important to remember that both are emotional attachments in the Now. Personal suffering as a perceived reality is an incorrect perception of the earth world, and also of the spirit world. There is no suffering, there is only change and transformation.

Bliss is also only a wave of feeling. We have discussed this before. Bliss is a cleansing, healing, light-filled wave, yet it is also a wave.

None of you, perhaps one or two, will be able to harness the energy of bliss for continual, continuous usage. This is a lesson you are learning.

What can be done is to shed the negative, and to continually purify yourself of the suffering, the violence, the anger, the hatred, and to continually turn away from this aspect.

Jesus said turn the other cheek, and by this he meant not to receive more pain, but instead to turn away fully, to refrain from participating, to allow no more of this dark force. By this he meant to shun the experience.

Other great beings have brought this message. These great messengers and teachers all chose the path of nonviolence, the path of love, the path of turning the other cheek—not to receive more, but to show that they do not participate in these acts of violence, anger, the hot steaming energy that prevails so much in your world.

For those who are especially sensitive to suffering, we ask that you call upon us continually and incessantly, that you never stop praying to us, for the world, for all beings, and that you bolster the world with your prayer and your connection to the Divine.

For those of you who seek bliss as entertainment, we ask that you recognize that it is only through continued and continual immersion in bliss that you can grow. By this we mean there is no growth in holding bliss one day, through meditation, singing, dance, or prayer—and then in visiting the other side and dowsing yourself with dark and lower energies of addiction, lust.

Suffering and bliss; these are both sides of the same coin. Suffering and bliss; both are the same. But you must choose which aspect you will experience, over and over and over. This is a point in your soul growth. This is the decision you must make. The dark or the light. The hate or the love. The anger or the compassion. The fight or the forgiveness. The chaos or the peace. You must continually choose in life's lesson, and you must make this choice constantly and continually with your soul, your mind, your body.

We do not speak of morals. We speak only of energy. Morals are confusing to you because they have been captured by those who use them as a methodology of controlling your mind. Morality has been captured by religions and companies, by groups and cults, so they might tell you what you should think and do.

You do not require this instruction from anyone or any group. Your soul cannot be controlled; it is God.

We speak of energy, of connection to the higher vibration of light and love, or of the lower vibration of what is dark. The light is what allows soul growth. You must choose this at every point of choosing that is set before you.

## Exercise

1. Write deeply of a time in which you made the choice between dark and light. We do not speak of morals. We speak of energies—light and dark, higher and lower vibrations.

2. Write deeply of the morals that you believe in or that you have been told you should believe in.

3. Write if you actually believe these are true.

4. What if they were not?

# Karmic destiny with others.

~

## CONSTANCE

My DARLINGS, THERE ARE MANY loves in this life. What you term as soul mate is actually any being with whom you have a karmic connection.

When you come across a person with whom you have shared a karmic state, you may remember that these states number a million, trillion, whatever is the highest number you can imagine. There are spiderweb-like pieces of energy that bind your soul to another's, and when you see this, you recognize this connection.

There is recognition.

Yes, we are connected All to All. There is no degree of separation between you and another. But with some souls, you meet and you continue to meet again and again, until you have received your karmic lesson—the lesson that is between you.

By this we mean, you meet until you are able to move beyond.

You may find this a sad idea—that once you have received your karmic lesson from another soul, then your karmic connection is complete.

This is just the way of it.

Thus, it is true that when you search for love, you must search for those you recognize. Those who you have karmic connection with may appeal to your earth eyes, your earth heart. Or, you may be attracted by those having similar features or characteristics to the ones with whom you have karmic destiny. It may be as simple as a physical characteristic, or a pattern of personality.

Yet there may be no karmic destiny between you at all.

Even something as unimportant as the way a person stands and moves may remind you of the one you knew in a previous life.

What is sure, is that when you do meet one with whom you share a karmic connection, the recognition is immediate. Many people have experiences of high voltage energy between themselves and this person. Many people have a mind connection that spans distances.

You may also have this karmic connection with those in your birth family, or in a family that you create, or you may not.

You may have this connection with friends, and this is mostly pleasant. This is your true family on earth.

You may also have this connection with a few, who are your karmic soul mates, in love.

You will note that we do not say there is only one. In the Bible, there is the idea of one man to one woman. This was during a time when earth beings did not live long. There was time only for one soul mating. In this time, you live longer. In the future, you will live longer still.

If love is also a part of the soul mating, it may last a lifetime. When love is not the lesson, but perhaps sex, power, forgiveness, pain, or the need to clear other karmic issues that lie between you, then the soul mating may exist and then be concluded.

Only when the field is based on love, will the soul mating be of the highest connection, for love is the highest creation we can aspire to.

You may find that you choose in this earth life not to have a primary love relationship. In this way you will share your love, with all the universe and all the plants, trees, animals, and other humans, even with every sip of cool air. This is a worthy path. This is available to all, even those who in the past would be expected to settle with another, raise children, without love, or without soul mating.

In this world, today in this world at this time, this is not required.

Sometimes you will meet a soul mate who is not ready for you. These people retain the karmic connection as a subtle thread of energy between you, until it is time for you to connect. This can be very disturbing to you if you are ready, and the other soul is not. Your choice is to wait for this other soul, or to move forward on to the next lesson that you will encounter. You may meet another soul mate at this time. You may not.

Love does not require soul mating.

Love requires love.

You will have the potential to choose to meet one, or perhaps a few, soul mates in your lifespan. There is not time for you to delve deeply in a connection with more than one or two, in the lifespan you have now. In later times, it may be that you choose a soul mate at the beginning, the middle, and the end of your life.

You will notice we do not talk of sex. Sex is a function of recreation, of lust, of energy, of the earth nature of the human. It is also a connective force, as some of you may have experienced; it can be the essence of the complete creation energy.

We do not confuse sex with love.

Sex is a part of the world for humans as it is for animals, for flowers, for trees, for all living things that reproduce themselves. You are not so different from other living creatures.

Sex with love is a gift, and should be cherished for the energy that passes from one to another. Sex without love is simply sex without love. Do not mistake the two. Do not pretend one is the other. Look clearly at your earth body and your infinite soul, and understand the difference.

If it should happen that you do meet more than one soul mate in one lifetime, be glad. You are nearing a point of learning that will transform you and move you into the next phase. Pay attention to these connections. When you have learned your lessons with one person, please clearly move forward. We are all connected. It is of no benefit to hold on to what is completed.

All souls are fluid, infinite, expansive, moving, growing. This is simply the way of souls: to grow further and to expand themselves infinitely.

Again, we say: do not become stuck. If you are stuck, move your soul forward. Let your earth heart contain the pain that is required to do this task, and continue in your lessons.

Now, we ask that you consider those whom you believe are soul mated to you. We ask that you close your eyes, and you bring the face of each person into your own field of remembrance, and we ask that you carefully consider this person. When you have achieved connection with them in your mind, ask them: are you a soul mate? Or were you a soul mate? And let yourself hear their answers.

Do not pass judgment. Do not force an answer from one with whom you only have an earth connection, not a soul connection. Do not attempt to create an answer because of the longing of your heart.

If there is no soul mating, let this be.

If there are several soul matings in your field, consider the timing for each, and where you are now in relation to each. The necessity of choosing between two soul mates—of two soul mates appearing at the same time—is very unlikely. The universe provides what you need in the time you need it.

With earth matings, choice is constant.

With soul matings, recognition is clear.

It is possible to love without soul mating. It is possible to have sex without soul mating. It is possible to have soul mating without being together for more than the briefest time.

It is possible for you to recognize your soul mate, and yet your soul mate may not be ready to move forward with you.

All of these are places which hold the earth heart, which fill the earth heart full and allow the earth heart to grow and enlarge in compassion, grief, and love. These are also your lessons.

## Exercise

1. Consider your soul mates—those you have called forward in your mind—and write each one's name. Now, allow your heart to expand and unfold in compassion for each of these people, and then to the entire group as a whole, and then toward all people on earth, and toward all beings in the universe.

2. If there is a new soul mating in your field, ask to be directed to this new person.

## LESSON TWENTY-FIVE

# Fame, fortune, power, possessions.

### CONSTANCE

*I AM BACK, AND READY to receive. I am more nervous now, because it has been nearly a month since I came to you. I am worried there will be nothing there.*

(Laughter.) My dear one. There is more for us to tell you than can be amassed in the writing of all the books and files on earth. There is both more for us to tell you, and nothing for us to tell you—it is an unending stream of guidance, and you may dip your hand in this stream at any time.

Today we speak only the message of peace.

By peace we mean the ability to be happy at any time, without regard to the markers you hold for success.

Not all of you long for success. Some of you long only for survival, and we say to you that you can move beyond this with just the nod of your head. There is only the limit of your imagination in this stage. To move from survival into success is as easy as wishing for it. You call this manifesting, and in this, we say yes, manifest from survival into success. It is here, at this juncture, when you have mastered survival, that you may begin to consider what is deemed success by your culture: fame, fortune, power, material items, wealth, sex appeal.

240

By power, we mean power of corporation, power of kinds, power of influence, physical power, power of holding dominion over another. By money we mean excessive money, either hoarded in gold or hoarded in bank, or even now as you hoard on credit, imagining you have wealth. So too is all money hoarded in banks—money is only tallies on paper or in electronica—so simple to whisk away with the breath of our breath, one simple thought and it is gone. We find that working with wealth and money in electronica is easy for us, and we have brought money to many of you simply and easily through this methodology. We do what is required, regardless of methodology.

When you hoard, there is always the fear that you will experience shortfall, that the wealth will disappear.

We say to you, this is not a bad thing.

For those of you who hold power, in all the ways you can hold power, there is always the danger that your power will disappear.

We say to you, this is not a bad thing.

For those of you who seek and hold fame, this is the most fickle power of all. You cannot capture the minds of any one save yourself, and (laughter) there is often the truth that you cannot capture your own mind.

Fame is one day glistening and bright, a glowing orb, a brilliant mirror. The next day it is anxiety—no one is looking at you, the telephone call is not received, no one pays court.

Fame is fickle, and it is ephemeral; it is all imagination. There is no person so famous that everyone admires this person; no being who controls through fame. Even we, who are of the angelic realm, who are known by those who seek us, and who are unlimited beings—we do not hold fame.

Fame is especially illusionary, and you must resist its captivation.

Some of these things—fortune, power, fame—are what you desire; also you desire material wealth. When you amass a large collection of material items, and by this we mean cars, boats, clothing, shoes, makeup, gadgetry, furniture, dishes, collections and so on—it is true that the more you want, the more you will have. The problem will be that you exist in the footprint of your beautiful home, and you do not know how to fill your day. Or you exist in the footprint of your beautiful home, and you grasp even more toward your satisfaction.

It is not wrong to have a beautiful home. But please see it for what it is.

It is not required.

At times in your life a home will be important, but at other times, a home will be the least of what you need. You will find your home in other places besides physical setting, objects, and collections. This idea of home as stability, permanence, changelessness—none of this is true. Home is nonexistent within a structure, or within the items inside that structure. Only the relationships in a home will satisfy—the true connection of one to another is where home is found.

This is the home that resides in your earth heart.

And yet, a safe, physical place to sleep, to be warm, to cook, to reside, to gather. This is your birthright as a physical being in the world. Surely a tree spreads a canopy over itself, and is safe for the night. A small bird finds its nest. Home in this sense is a true home: a place where you can rest and be loved.

But home in the sense of furniture, car, boat, lawns watered and saturated with pesticide and poison, the home as a competition within the neighborhood, or amongst one's friends and relatives—the home as showplace. This is no home.

Many of you have the addiction of shopping. Shopping is no worse or better than any of the other addictions, but it is an addiction and comes from the same source, which is fear and pain.

What drives you is the desire.

Or, you may value items overmuch, like the child who keeps all his toys on the shelf, never using them in play, or the woman who keeps her clothing protected in bags and boxes, never wearing them in her real life.

Or the man who keeps a collection of cars, or instruments, or fine wines, whatever it is he collects, who displays these objects as a measure of his success, his wealth, or his ability to manifest what he desires.

What is not enjoyed has no worth.

We return to the subjects of fortune, power, fame. These are the measures of success on the earth, yet these are unable to bring you peace.

Peace of the earth heart—this is what your soul longs for.

When we say you are perfect, that your soul is perfect—it is. You are. But your earth heart, in all its perfect imperfection, causes you all kinds of misery, and this is misery you may choose to be without—this misery does not bring happiness.

Your earth heart does not long for sadness. It longs for peace. Your earth heart is not about being a neutral force—no, we say to you: enjoy your life on earth, enjoy your earth heart, for it is the most dazzling force of all, for all the love and sorrow it can contain. The joy and compassion of which you are immensely capable. This is your process, to grow your earth heart so that it encompasses all without boundaries, so it is as eternal and infinite as your perfect soul of One.

Thus, we say this: consider that fortune, power, fame, the amassing of material items—that these can never satisfy.

For those of you who are still afraid, who continue to seek and gather material items, who amass, for those of you who strive for markings of success, who cannot imagine life without all that surrounds you—we say to you, this is a trap, a box, a prison, There is no way you can move beyond, if you are held down by these things.

And yet the first step is terrifying. The first releasing is beyond endurance.

This is why we are here to help you, with glowing light, with infinite support and assistance.

Just say the words "help me," and we are there in a rush of wings. We are there. And we say this to you, and to you, and to you, and to you. There is no one we do not come to, regardless of their earth deeds. No one.

## Exercise

Consider in your mind, in prayer and meditation, your position, in terms of addiction. By addiction, we mean:

- Fame
- Fortune
- Power
- Material possessions

We ask that you consider who you are, without these addictions.

1.  Fame. If you hold fame, please write your worst fears if you find that suddenly you are without fame.
2.  Please write ten ways you are free, without fame. Please write all ten.
3.  Fortune. Please list ten things you could immediately divest yourself of, right now.
4.  Write how this makes you free.
5.  Power. List the people and companies and groups you have power over.
6.  Write how releasing yourself from the need to hold power sets you free.

We instruct you that the earth heart longs to be whole. The earth heart longs to be enormous, huge in its compassion and generosity and connection. The earth heart longs to be a universe of love. All things that impede, that misdirect, that trick or trap—you are not required to hold these.

# Slavery to time is not required by you.

⟶

## CONSTANCE

In this Lesson we will speak of the days. You have so many days in your earth life. Some of you have a few left. Some of you may have many days, so many that they seem countless. Of course, this is not true. All things are measurable, except for what is eternal and infinite.

Your soul is eternal and infinite.

Your earth life is finite.

This is no mystery to you.

All of you have seen death, which is the extinguishing of your earth life. When the flame of your earth life is doused, it exists no more. You, as an eternal soul, continue on as infinite, one of One.

But your earth life is precious, and your days are numbered.

In this way you are very much like the leaves that fall with the seasons, that turn golden, red, brown, and display the height of their beauty, then drop forth from the tree, to be scattered around your feet. The tree does not die, only the leaves. So too do you die your earth death, whereas your soul, the tree, continues to live.

But in your earth life there are limited days.

And so we ask you, how do you spend your days?

⬦

Your schedules are a form of slavery. And yet to what end?

You tear yourself from sleep, you use drugs and chemicals to allow yourself to pace this schedule. You are a slave to the minute, the hour, the day. Without schedule you are unable to think your own thoughts clearly, or even to know your own thoughts. Your schedule enslaves you as surely as you might be a slave to another, in a past time.

You allow this—you are like sheep. But we say: do not be led by leaders. Do not be led by culture. Do not be led by schedule. Lead yourself. Do not allow your earth body, your earth heart, your earth self, to be shackled as slave to time.

Time is the most illusionary force of all. Time stops still in an instant, or it extends forever. Time extends, it spins, it reverts on itself, it is infinitely paralleled past, present, future, all in the same moment.

You may choose to exist in whatever flow of time that you prefer.

Slavery to time is not required by you.

And yet you arrive in panic, even now your thoughts and voices arise in panic. For time, the schedule, the slavery, this is the biggest addiction of all. You are addicted to the schedule, to the illusion of forward movement in time; you cling to this, because you believe it will give your life meaning.

We say: let your schedules go. Let them crash around your knees. Give yourself no schedule. Allow yourself all time. And once you have broken through the initial panic, the initial fear of who you are—then you will begin to live with your earth heart.

When you were a child, and you lived full in your body and in your experience—time meant nothing. You did not require yourself to be anywhere, to do anything.

Now, when you first sit without time, you will find that is a strain to be still. We do not speak even of meditation, or prayer. We speak merely of sitting, outside of time.

When you sit, when you allow time to wash over you, verily, as a wave—when you allow the pain and bliss of time to wash over you—you begin to realize that time has no measure.

Fast, slow . . . it is the same. Past, present, future . . . there is no difference.

◆

We understand that this idea is very hard for you. It goes across the ideology that you have been taught, which is incorrect. Time is not linear. Time is all-expansive, all around you. It is like a globe of shimmering energy that surrounds you. You may choose any direction in this infinite energy—up, down, forward, back, even directions that you do not know the name for. You are at the center, you are at the corner, you are at the edge, you are at the outermost part, which extends infinitely. This is your earth body in time.

It is not a linear line.

What is infinite is you, and what is infinite is everything. There is no line or hemisphere dividing the infinite, the complete density of time.

This idea is not understood by most of you. We feel it may be too difficult; beyond what the earth body can realize at this point. Still, we say to you: do not consider time as linear. Know that it is Something Else. And for this reason consider yourself as no longer shackled to time. Consider that there is another life, a more glorious earth life, if you take the key that you have in your pocket, verily unlock the shackles, and you slip away from this time lock, this slavery.

We hear your arguing, your clamoring, your panic, your fear. We say: within the limits of time, you can never be free.

Within the limits of time, you will always know the deep hunger that is never satisfied. Within the limits of time, you will always be racing in a race that cannot be won.

◆

In linear thought, all time ends in death.

Yet in the realm that we speak of, death does not end. Death is only a change, a transformation from one state to the other. Like a baby being born, entering the world—so too is death a birth that you will not experience until it is your own moment of transformation.

Death does not end—it is a transformation.

And this, knowing that this transformation will occur to you, and to you, and to you, is one of the things you may depend upon in your life. Not that you will die, but that you will be transformed. Thus, you may consider that all things leading up to your death—your transformation—are worthy of your attention.

The life of slavery does not appeal to many.

The life of slavery is not a life worth living.

The life of slavery does not have to be your choice.

In the past, slaves were indentured to others, and there is still this now in your world. But for those of you who have moved beyond survival, to that of success, we ask: why are you still a slave?

This Lesson will cause consternation, and we insist that you answer these questions. There is no more clear methodology to saving your life. And by saving your life, we mean living free, living with an enormous, infinitely huge earth heart filled with compassion, and love, delight and joy, rapture and happiness. An earth heart that is so big that it expands over and over again; there is no end to how big your earth heart can expand, or how much love and compassion you may be filled with.

## Exercise

1. Consider your day. This day. Write your schedule for this day.

We advise you that there is nothing for you to do. There is no place for you to go. You may do as you please.

2. Write now what you would do with one such day.

3. Write now what you would do with two days.

4. Write now what you would do in a year, in which you were free, and had all the time you needed.

# You are what you do.

## CONSTANCE

IT SEEMS JUST LAST WEEK *was April*.

This is the case, when time turns on itself.

*It seems impossible for time to move so quickly.*

Again, we say time is illusion. You have as much or as little time as you need. This is why we ask you to look at time as nonlinear, so that you may utilize it better for your own soul growth and happiness.

❖

You are what you do. This is true for you, and for all of you. You are what you do. Your thoughts create destiny but it is your feet that carry you forward. For example, if you desire a certain thing to come to pass, then you may indeed think it into existence. But without action accompanying this desire, nothing will happen.

Action is putting intent into the universe. Thought also creates intent; action may be perceived as stronger thought.

You are what you do. If you are an artist, if you envision and manifest yourself as an artist, and if you paint or create art daily or often, regardless of your ability, then you are an artist in your life.

If you are a banker, you are not an artist. If you are a farmer, you are not an artist. If you are a mother, and spend all your time mothering while dreaming of being an artist—this is not an artist.

You are what you do.

Thus if you wish to be an artist, you must be an artist.

This is true in a broader sense also. If you wish to be happy, then you must be happy. If you wish to experience bliss, then you must be in bliss.

Thus, if you are anxious, depressed, addicted, poor, abused, all of these things that create misery for you . . . your mind has settled you there. But it is both thought and action that break this lock, that open the door of these traps.

This is so simple, and yet so many of you continue to call on us in prayer, or continue to call to us with longing, saying, "Please help me." We are with you at all times. But because of your own will, that which is free will, we can only assist you when we are also assisted by you, in action.

If you wish to be free from drinking, you must ask for help, you must create action by stopping drinking, and you must pray for support. This is the way that this will become.

If you wish to be free from depression, you must ask for help from us, and you must stop being depressed. By this we mean you must rise up, you must become involved, you must open your heart to another, you must claim the fierce love inside you and pour it out for the world to see. And you must ask for support from us again and again.

Depression comes from lack of connection. It is not from stress. It is not from imbalance in the body. For most of you, it is simply from lack of connection within your heart's life, your earth heart's life.

Change does not happen over time. Change happens in an instant. Change happens at the point of asking for help; it happens when you in your mind ask to receive change. Even if you are unable to see change at this point, change has happened. Change has happened from the moment of asking us, the Holy Ones, to work in the energy of now. This is the way in which your thoughts become your action.

You are what you think.

You also are what you do.

Your thoughts become your actions.

Your actions are supported by asking us for help.

If you are a writer, you must write.

If you are priest, you must preach.

If you are a cook, you must cook.

If you are a teacher, you must teach.

If you do not know your life's purpose yet, we say to you: listen. Your life's purpose is already ingrained in you; it is as fused to you as a seaweed clings to the rocks. You have seen this: how seaweed wraps the rock and eventually covers it, so the rock itself cannot be seen.

Your life's path, your life's purpose, is what is required by your perfect soul, for your perfect soul's growth. It is measured by your earth heart's growth.

The ability to see beauty, to have compassion, to know what it is to give and to receive love, to enlarge your heart so much that it contains room for all of humanity, and then to ask to receive more—to make room for all of the Holy Ones, for room to place yet another Jesus in your heart, yet another Mohammed, yet another saint or ascended master, and then to add in all the other Holy Ones in the universe, even who you do not know of yet, but who some of you will know in time. To continue to add in everyone—friend, family, enemy, into your heart, until your heart is filled to bursting.

And then to add another.

And to do all of this without fear, my friend. Without fear. To continually open your heart.

For the earth heart bends and breaks, and the earth heart can be wounded, but in each measure of this exists the intention and possibility of it becoming larger, to enlarge itself until it is the size of the universe, which as you know is unlimited and unending.

Thus, your life's purpose is this. Your life's path is this. To expand your heart until it is the size of the universe. Any other measure of your life's path—as to what is your calling, what should you do—this is deeply given to you, for you are unique in your talents and your abilities that you may give to the world.

You may affect many, you may affect a few. The number is not what is important.

But you must walk in the world with your earth heart ever compassionate and ever expanding, growing bigger with each day, growing bigger always, and you must do this without fear.

This is the purpose of your life.

All beings will not connect back with you. All beings will not open to you. Many will harm you, many will break you, many will cause you great pain. This is the way of the earth heart. But we again ask you to hold your heart open with compassion. To open your earth heart, and to also take this person in—the enemy, the one who shuns you, the one who has offended you, the one who is hurtful.

This is not forgiveness, for it is not your place to forgive.

This is compassion, for it is the state of human existence that you are perfect souls with imperfect bodies—earth hearts that must struggle to learn.

If you desire soul growth, you must allow the opening and the expansion of your earth heart.

## Exercise

1. Write down a list of people with whom you would like to have connection. We do not mean romance, sex, lust. We mean simply, people with whom you would like to have connection.

2. Now, write down the names of those who you have no connection with; those who have hurt your heart, or who have caused you pain.

Remember, forgiveness is not your affair. It is only showing compassion that is within your scope and realm. We ask that you consider these people on your life's path, and that you open your heart to hold them.

# LESSON TWENTY-EIGHT

# The true hero quests within.

⟶

## CONSTANCE

FEAR IS WHAT HOLDS YOU back from the purpose of your life, which is heart's learning, which is soul growth.

It is the fear of your earth heart breaking.

We say: the heart cannot break. The heart is unlimited in its ability to take pain, to feel compassion, to generate connection, to contain and exude love.

But if you have been walking with a closed, sealed heart, if you have been walking in this life with a closed heart, then you will be afraid. You have been carrying your heart like a brilliant, cold gem in your chest, and it is true that your heart is treasure. Yet it is also true that if you hoard it away like precious gem, it becomes smaller and smaller.

The heart is infinite. It is meant to expand.

So we ask—do you prefer to have a ruby-bright heart that sparkles and is rich with depth and glow, that is yours alone, only to be enjoyed by you, yet is shrinking smaller each day, until it is the last and only treasure you hold?

Or do you wish for an expansive heart that knows no bounds, or no limits?

What holds you back is fear.

What releases you is courage.

The true hero quests within.

There is no dragon to slay. There is no war to win. There is no mountain to climb. There is only the landscape of what is within, which is you in the universe. Which is you as one of the now of the Now. Which is also you, as an earth being, with an earth heart, surrounding and infinitely connected to all living beings.

Thus, the hero's quest is for no chalice, no sword, no banner. The hero's quest in this time is for connection; it is for compassion, it is for love.

This is the task of this world you are in now.

There is much work to be done.

Many in your world will be unable to make this shift. We do not judge who will or who will not. It is the choice that is important.

We ask that you choose without fear.

We ask that you let fear wrap you and stain you and corrupt you, and then you discard fear.

We ask that you look at fear, in all its forms: anxiety, depression, stagnation, living dead in the world, holding yourself back, illness, addiction, wealth, ambition—all of these are ways of assuaging your need not to feel fear.

We say: let yourself know the fear.

Many of you fear death. Yet death is simply a passing to the next. The souls move in stages, and the process is gentle. You will have what you need when your time comes. There is nothing to fear in this way.

Do you fear the measure of your life? We say: measure is not important. Neither is time. What is done is not important, only what is felt and given. The money, the possessions, the competitions, the degrees, the collections, the fame, the sexual conquests, the addictions, the travel, the things you have done, these forces are outer. These are dust on the wind.

What is important is your heart's growth, its compassion, and your ability to connect.

We do not say this, as some of you believe, as measure of being without sin, or of being saved. These terms do not have place with us. These terms are misused, have been misinterpreted in your books, and by your leaders.

There is nothing to be saved—you are saved already. This is the way of the universe.

Jesus did not come to save; Jesus came to teach the ways of the earth heart. What has been written and said is misinterpretation.

There is no need for forgiveness; forgiveness is not in our lexicon.

There is only need for connection, for compassion, for love.

There is only need for connection, compassion, and love.

When you see that you are not only alongside your brother, but that you are your brother—this is when you begin to become happy. When you see that you are not from your mother, but that you are also your mother—this is when your heart grows.

There is no other purpose than love.

There is no other path than soul growth.

You may resist, you may avoid, you may be paralyzed with fear—for some of you this is your entire life. You may be paralyzed in fear, not acting, not doing, not feeling. You may be holding the brittle diamond or ruby that is your heart, holding it safe inside your heart as a locked treasure.

But we say: unlock the treasure chest. Take your heart out, in all its faceted brilliance, and then throw it on the table. Give it away.

Do this without fear.

If you have fear, do it anyway.

Open your heart up, throw the gem on the table, and watch how your earth heart expands, swells, becomes larger and larger, softens and deepens, how it can hold more, and allow more and more to be

held, even as it shines brighter and brighter until the world is illuminated with the brilliance and great tenderness of your earth heart.

This is the way to save the world.

Fear is not needed by you. You may release it at any time. You may
release fear in its entirety.

If you are afraid of death, we say: do not fear death. Death is not a
worry for you.

If you hold fears of measures in your life, do not hold onto these. In
one moment of connection, your life becomes real. This is the greatest
achievement of your life: your compassion, connection, your love.

Compassion. Connection. Love.

## Exercise

1. Write down your fears.

2. Now, imagine that these fears may be released, and write down
   which fears you would like to be released. This is done before
   the moment you have asked.

3. Now that your fears are gone, we ask that you consider the
   minutes you have left in your earth life. Write down what is
   the best use of your heart.

# Rest in this magnificence.

~

## GABRIEL

SIT WITH ME FOR A moment now. I would like you to feel the healing that is available to you, at any time. Some of you have felt this as glowing, golden—this is the color and warmth of God. It is light, it is energy. It is direct healing for you.

Sit with me for a moment, quietly, and let your soul commune with mine, for verily we are One.

Breathe simply. Close your eyes, and feel the peace seeping into your heart. You will feel it first in your heart, for this is where God comes to you.

In your eyes, in your ears, in your mouth, and on your lips. But mostly God comes to you in your heart, for this is where you feel the glowing, golden presence.

Sit with me, and you will know God.

Sit with me, and you are healed.

You may drink of the cup that is God, drink as much as you like, there is no end. The chalice brims. The cup runneth over. My cup runneth over, you have said in times past. You. By this we mean specifically you, Scribe, and also you and you. There is nothing more than to drink of the golden, inexhaustible, infinite, complete whole, the entire luscious liquid of this cup that is God, and feel this seep into your heart, and be quenched, and feel this saturate every part of your body, with golden infinite glow. This is the Now.

Drink of the Now that is God.

Sit with me, bask in this, soak it in, fill yourself up with it. Luxuriate and gravitate and fall and be resplendent. Soak and be stirred and allow yourself to fall fully into this.

This is your God. This is the you, the One, this is your Now—it is all the same, it is all holy, you are as much a part of our own Being, Divine as All, as Divine as any of the Holy Ones, as Divine as any of the gods' names.

Sit with me. I am part of you. Many of you have known my name— but know me now. I have come to many of you, and others have come to others of you, and we invite you to soak up and sup, and revel in the glory of the golden holiness.

Sit with me a minute now, and let me seep into your body. Sit with me, and let me place my hands upon your head, and let yourself feel the energy that comes from me, that is received by you, and that you may in turn provide to another.

Sit with me, and rest in this magnificence.

It is the easiest thing you will ever find; it is the only thing that is important. Connect with God, connect with God and with each other. Bring yourself into full force of God, without shame, without fear, for your soul is perfect, your earth heart is open and filling and ever expansive.

There is no need for transformation. You have already been transformed.

There are no questions for this Lesson.

Rest in this magnificence. Let us rest in this together.

# Turning compassion into love.

‑⊖‑

## GABRIEL

*GABRIEL, I ASK IF IT is you who appears, because I have heard your name,
and I have received your messages, but I am questioning if this is you, and
if I have heard from you already.*

Yes, I am the source of comfort. I appear to you as young, and I
come to you as a young voice because your own voice is young; in
this way we mirror each other. Even the young voice has a mighty
message and sound. Even the young, sweet voice of comfort is God at
all levels, not only the voice of power or the voice of destruction.

We say to you all, lift your voices. The sweet voices are the ones
that soothe the heart; the tender, gentle voices; the voices of Mother;
the voices of comfort; the voices of love in the quiet moments. Love
between man and woman, love in all ways, but also love as love from
friend to friend. The simple love of you to a flower, a tree.

In the simple, soft, and gentle ways, your heart feels relief; it feels
calm. Like a baby held in its mother's arms.

Yes, I have come to you, with such love, with such longing to express the beauty of the world, but coming in gently, like the soft breath
of air, coming in gently, so that you will not be afraid. Thus you have
already spoken to me many times, as I am there and in the moment
for each person who calls my name.

There are others of us who come with great blaze of trumpets, shouts of Gloria and Hosanna. I come this way to some, but for most I arrive as a gentle breath. I bring comfort to the heart that is in pain. I am the cool hand on your brow. I am the soft words that you long to hear; I am your most tender thoughts. In this way, I remind you what it is to be tender, what it is to be open.

You know already that an open heart holds pain. An open heart, kept open, feels pain. This is the way in which you know compassion. When you keep your heart open, my dear ones, your heart may collect pain from the others around you. You notice this person's unhappiness, or that person's longing or craving—and your heart knows the hopelessness. Misery is hopelessness; there is no answer in misery. But your heart sees the pain and wants to assuage it for another.

When the open heart sees the pain of the other, the pain is transferred.

It is for all of you who take on the pain of another that I come. I come especially for the children, for those who are young in spirit, for those who were born open and who do not know how to close, for those who have opened recently.

Remember: the opening of the heart can happen instantly.

Do you see how easy my words are upon your ear? There is nothing to fear.

So if you will call on me at this time, when you have taken on the pain of another, and I will come and clear you with golden light, with the sweet balm of my own being, you will be cleared. It is effortless. You will just call me, Gabriel. And in a moment's notice, before the words have been spoken, I will come and I will heal you from this holding.

When you have pain in your own heart from memories, from past hurts and so forth, this is a releasing that I can help you with, but it is also a part of your soul lesson to release. If you have painful memories, memories of things that did not go as you liked, or where you were abandoned, or teased, or hated, such injury will cause our hearts to close.

If these have caused your heart to close, to become encrusted over with pain and with hiding and with shame—then this is for you to release.

Yet if you call on me, I will help you.

There is never a time that I will not help you, or the others of us. It is our greatest joy to heal a heart, a heart that is brave and wishes to be cleared from pain.

It is for you to hold compassion in your heart, for this is what makes you human. But at the same time, once you have compassion, you are ready to move to the next step—to know the radiance of love.

Again. When you hold compassion for another's pain, you must release this compassion into love.

And if you hold onto your own pain, in the form of memories and past hurts, revenge and anger, then it is also necessary for you to release this pain, shame and anger into love.

In this way, your heart is healed.

After a while, and many of you do this already, your heart becomes continually at peace. As pain is noticed, it is felt deeply and with compassion, and it is recreated in love.

This is the simplest thing.

And what is to be remembered is that you may call on me, Gabriel. And I will appear not with trumpets or wings, but with soothing joy. Even now you feel my great love for you.

Especially ask us to heal what is past. When you are a child, the past has not entwined you. But now that you are not a child, what is past roams around in your memory, overlapping, underlying, great cordings of memory and confusion, belief and structure, great cordings of thought and distraction.

You cannot have your feet in both past and present—one foot on the bank of the river, one foot in the river. To be alive, to be living and growing with open heart and brimming light, both feet must be in the river, the river that sails effortlessly on.

You may call on me. There is no time that I will not come: Gabriel. In this same way, there is no time that any of us, the ascended, will not come. If you call on your ancestors, they will come as they can. But if you call on the ascended, thousands of us from the angelic plane will come before you have asked. If you call on these ascended masters, avatars, angels, and others who roam the earth, they are there before their names are uttered.

You may also call on the spirits of nature. A great tree, a soaring bird. These beings are sacred; they are not human, but they hold great energies. In trees, you will find great comfort and love. In the animal realm, you will find a pure energy that is Now. In the rocks, and sands of the desert, you will find holy space.

Remember, when you call us, the healing is already complete. In the act of calling upon us, the healing is done.

## CONSTANCE

Here are the questions for this Lesson. We ask that you breathe in, breathe out, and that you fill your heart with the greatest light.

## Exercise

1. Is your heart open? How much?

2. Do you take on another's pain? What residue is there from the pain of war, violence, or the noticing of another's pain?

3. What past memories or lifestyles or actions have damaged your heart?

We ask next that you sit quietly, and ask for the pain to be cleared. We are with you in light; there is no end to when we are with you.

# The heart is meant to transform pain into love.

~☞~

### GABRIEL

AGAIN WE WOULD RETURN TO this Lesson of transforming the heart. When the heart is filled with pain, the heart can contain all of the pain of the universe. But the heart is not meant to hold pain in a static way.

The heart is meant to transform the pain it holds into love.

This is the point at which you may have confusion. To walk with compassionate heart, or hurt heart, or broken heart—all of these are one step of your growth. But to transform a heart of pain into a heart of compassion into a heart of love—this is what we are asking.

It is not hard for you to do this, but you must believe. A bird does not believe it can fly, but yet it does, and this is a miracle. A fish does not believe it can swim, and yet it does. You do not know that your heart can transform pain into love, yet it can.

However, this process requires you to accept even more pain, and to open your heart bigger and wider than you have opened it before. When your heart is fully opened to its biggest capacity, so big that you feel it cannot contain all the pain and all the compassion, it is here that grace begins to appear.

Pain to compassion to love.

Pain to compassion to love.

The greatest gift to the world is the lightness of your heart, the love in your heart, the pure love emanating from you like golden beams. Light and love pours from you; the pain that once hollowed you and spread like a bruise upon you is miraculously healed in the heart of golden light.

In this way you are filled with the energies that we operate from, the light forces.

The part that is hard for most of you is not the opening of the heart the first time, which most of you have already experienced. It is the second opening that is difficult—when the heart is ready to crack or burst from so much pain or compassion. It is here the transformation of grace occurs. It is here that the heart changes from one energy into another.

The blazing of light from this heart is unmistakable.

Again, and we say this many times so you will attend us—it is not enough to open your heart to feel pain. It is not enough to open your heart further to feel compassion, which is a step beyond pain. It is by opening your heart yet again a second time, to its fullest, most open aspect, and to allow the compassion—yes, the compassion—to be lifted from you and transformed into love.

These concepts are new to you. You have been taught that the compassionate heart—that this was the heart of grace. Yet we say: the heart must be bursting with not just compassion, but transformed by grace into pure love.

This is the heart of light.

To receive the light of the Divine and of the Holy Father, the Holy Mother, of all that is unseen and glorious, please ask for grace, please allow us to open your heart wider each day, and to bring the gift of grace to you.

The saints and the Holy Ones burn with the heart of light. You who are saints already also have this light burning. You who are compassionate are ready to move to the next plane. You who feel only pain—we will show you the gift of compassion. You who feel anger, we will give you the gift of pain. In each stage, the heart is opened fuller, until the grace of true light and true love fills every portion of the heart, the body, the mind, extending in all directions and filling your being at all times and all planes.

## CONSTANCE

In time you will understand that the heart is mixed in what it contains. Pain, compassion, pure love, and light may all coexist. This is the process of the human earth heart. As you become filled with grace, your heart will experience pure light more often.

## Exercise

1. Please write ways in which your heart feels pain.

2. Please write as many ways in which your heart feels compassion.

3. Please write ways in which your heart feels pure love.

# Transcend bliss to grace.

⟶

## GABRIEL

TO BE IN A STATE of grace is different from the state of bliss. Again, bliss is a method of matching your earth body's energy to the universe.

Imagine if a stone becomes a hummingbird. One has a slow energy; the other has a fast energy. The energy of the universe, of God, the Father, is deep and immense and different than the energy of your earth body. When you are able through prayer, meditation, music and singing, connection with another, to achieve a state of bliss, it is a matching of your energy to the universe.

This state of grace—bliss with love—this is a transcendent force.

But whereas bliss is a pathway to grace, it is not in itself complete.

Many of you in earth bodies have become as addicted to bliss as to any of the other addictions in your world. It is easy to meditate for hours and to match your vibration to the universe. This is neither bad nor good. Like the universe, all energy is the present moment; it is what it is.

But to transcend bliss and enter a state of divine grace—this is the moment when the earth body connects and matches the universal presence of love.

It is a fine difference.

But it is the difference between a stone and a hummingbird.

---

Bliss allows you to see God.

Grace allows you to become One with God.

---

How do you know if you are experiencing pure light and love? Love is not exclusive. It is all around you, without exception. Love does not discriminate. It makes no difference to love who is what, or who is why. There is only love and light, emanating from all beings, and to all beings. It is the ultimate generosity, the ultimate homage and selflessness. It is both given and received simultaneously.

Pure love is not given to only one other; it must be given to all, including your own earth self. Such is the power of pure love.

In your earth body, you say you love this one or that one . . . this is earth love. In pure love, there is no specific. There is no discrimination; there is no one who is loved, and one who is not loved. Pure love emanates to all, without end.

Pure love is for all beings, every being. Even those beings that you do not perceive as being: wood, rock, earth, air. These are also infused with grace.

## Exercise

1. Write down whom you love, specifically. Those you love the most.

2. Please now pray for the blessings of these people.

3. Now, meditate on the state of grace that is true love. Consider how this love blazes through you, and is delivered to all. Consider how you are transcended by this state of grace. Consider how those who receive this love are also transcended.

# Your heart can hold everything.

## GABRIEL

COME, SIT WITH ME. YOU have been experiencing movement of time, fluxation in your sense of time.

*Yes.*

This is the normal process of how time moves. It can be confusing for you when you begin to reach this state but this is how time is fluid around you.

Time shifts as your vibration shifts. Because you have raised your vibration recently in the training you are taking, time has begun to appear to you more as it really is. It is fluid and without measure. The clocks you have ticking with each minute clicking onto the next—this is not time. The ideas you have of time in a linear way, of time existing one moment to the next, one time segment marching behind the other—this is not time.

You feel time as emotion now, is this not so?

*Yes.*

This is the closest way to how time really is.

When you meditate, or pray, or connect with us in the higher vibrations, your energy begins to match the energy of the Now and the One, which is a higher vibration than you are used to. There is a scale of vibration, as in music, as in sound, color, light, and as in time. There are many vibrations also beyond this, but most of you are not able to feel them all yet, although some of you do. There other energy forces that swirl around you at all moments, but you do not always feel them, or have the capability to feel them.

However, when you meditate or pray, or you receive the words from us, the vibrations in you shift and are raised. Often, when we come to you, we will move our vibration to match yours. This is something we do so that you can hear or see us more clearly. We are able to match you, and you are in some spaces available to match us, but this is more uncommon. In time, this skill will be known by all, but it is not yet this time.

Thus, you have noticed time exists in a new way for you. A moment feels full and complete, even though it only measured as a small segment of time. Especially as of late when you have been very involved with writing, with healing and with channeling, this fluidity that is measured as hours moves so quickly that four or five hours of what you measure as time passes as quickly as the blink of an eye.

Conversely, many days pass quickly, without awareness of how many, or how fast.

This is being in the Now, when you are so immersed, so entranced by what you are doing, that you do not notice the movement of time. You do not notice it, because time does not move. Time just is. It is the Now. It is always the Now.

When you are in the ultimate now of the Now, when you are one with the One, then time has no meaning.

Yet the other aspect of you that is most important is how your heart feels during time.

You do not experience time as segments, as matter, as anything, even though in your mind you hold it this way. You experience time only as the way your heart feels during that segment.

You understand there is no segment; there is only the Now. But we use this wording segment, to help you understand how it is in your earth body.

In your earth body, what is held in your heart is what you know as your experience. What you feel and know through the state of your emotions—this is how you define yourself.

When you feel pain, or fear, or anger, or any of the other baser emotions, you feel time either moving too quickly to experience it, as when you are feel a coursing rage of anger, or you feel time a slow stagnation—it is unbearable to you.

When you feel compassion, time seems to move more slowly, for compassion is tinged with pain. Time may drag or feel heavy to you.

If you are in bliss, you are in a very high vibration, and time appears to simultaneously be changeless and also moving very quickly. You have bonded and melded and become one with time, one with the Now, when you are in bliss.

If you are in pure love, this is the highest vibration, the ultimate Now, where time is not felt.

This is a state of Holiness for you.

The more you match your vibrations to higher frequencies, through meditation, in prayer, or by communicating and requesting the presence of us who can your raise your vibration, the more time stands still.

This you have been noticing, Scribe, as you are receiving our words.

Time is the Now, time is the One. There is no distinction. Once you understand that there is no distinction, that one is not separate from the other, that you are the same: you, the air; you, the rock; you the emotion; you the time; you the Now; you the One. It is all the same.

And yet. You have an earth body. And this reality of this slower vibration of living on earth, it is also a part of you.

Here is where the great Holiness of your lives, of you and you and you and you is found. Where you can hold the idea in your mind that you are earth body, and that you are also Holy Spirit.

Soul is eternal and unlimited. It is always connected. But in your earth body is where you must learn this lesson. Of being distinct, but also part. Of being of time, but also out of time. Of being in heavier vibration, but able to match higher vibration. Of holding emotion, but also realizing emotion is nothing more than air.

You have heard that your earth life is illusion, but do not misunderstand. Illusion implies that you do not need to care, that you do not need to walk with your earth heart open, brimming with compassion and love. Illusion implies that your existence in this earth life does not matter.

You matter.

The way you hold energy in your heart, the way you learn and grow and try—this is the most Holy task of all, to be both things: earth body and ephemeral spirit.

We say: you are the Holy Ones. You and you and you and you.

## Exercise

For this lesson, we ask that you open your heart and that you receive us. By us, we mean God, the One, the All, the Now. By us, we mean yourself. Allow your earth heart to brim with us, and know that you may hold an unlimited amount of pain, compassion, bliss, and love in your heart.

1. Please write that you are God. You may write: I am God.

2. Please write that there is no separation between you in your earth body, and you in your Holy Spirit.

3. Close your eyes, and rest with us, matching our vibration. Imagine yourself with all the Holy Ones.

4. Now imagine yourself in a group of friends or family—it does not matter who. Imagine their holiness, their infinite grace.

This grace and beauty is in each of you, and you, and you. There is no one this is not in, no matter how it maybe be covered, ravaged, hoarded. There is no one who is not Holy. There is no one who is not One.

❖

My dear ones. This particular set of lessons is ending. There is nothing more for you to know, except that your heart can hold everything. There is nothing more to know, except that you are One.

Let yourself fall into the river, and be carried away in the river of Now. You cannot keep one foot on the bank, and one foot in the river. Instead, you must submerge yourself in the river that is your earth life. Submerge yourself without fear, and allow yourself to be carried away by the water of your life.

Your earth life is a precious gift. We hear you, we watch you, we attend to you at all moments, for we know the struggles of the earth heart and the Holy Spirit; they coexist together.

We ask that you consider that which you see as important: schedules, distractions, addictions, money, success, education, power, fame, pride, associations, company, church, cult, organization.

All of this is unessential to you.

You exist as earth heart brimming with pain, compassion, love. You exist as perfect, pure soul.

We ask that you understand that there is no distinction between you and you and you and One.

If you are still afraid, please call upon us and ask for transformation in your heart.

If you are angry, please call on us,

If you are uncertain, please call on us,

If you are in stagnation, please call on us,

If you do not know what to do, please call on us.

We are there, bringing you light and love in that instant, before you have even said the words.

# Glossary

**Angel:** A Holy Being and messenger of God in Christian and other religions.

**Astral projection:** Ability to project one's consciousness to another place, time, or realm, while the body remains in the present reality.

**Automatic writing:** Term for channeled writing used by Spiritualists of the late 1800s and early 1900s.

**Automat:** Term for channeled writing used by Spiritualists of the late 1800s and early 1900s.

**Beloved:** Rumi's concept of the Beloved, both as God and as the lover or soul mate.

**Bliss:** An ecstatic state of transcendence.

**Brainstorming:** A creative tool that considers all solutions, good and bad, in hopes of finding a best solution.

**Buddha:** The ancient spiritual teacher and Holy One, Gautama Buddha.

**Chakra:** Sanskrit word meaning "circle or wheel," corresponding to seven energy centers in the body.

**Channeling:** The act of receiving information from another entity, through trance.

**Channeled writing:** Written messages received from another entity, through trance.

**Clairaudience:** The art of psychic hearing.

**Clairsentience:** The art of psychic feeling.

**Clairvoyance:** The art of psychic seeing.

**Conduit:** A channel through which something flows.

**Constance:** The first spirit guide to deliver The 33 Divine Lessons.

**Dass, Ram:** Author of groundbreaking spiritual book *Be Here Now*.

**Direct connection:** The concept of being able to make a direct, two-way connection with the Divine, without a third party or additional process.

**Divine:** God, the Now, Source, Presence, all names for the cosmic One.

**Downward Dog:** A yoga position.

**Entity:** A being, spirit, or presence that is not human.

**Five-year plan:** A common corporate and life-coaching concept, as in "Where do you want to be in five years?"

**Flow:** The constant, creative state of the universe. Also, the act of working with universal creative energy, Source, Presence, the Divine, the Now, One, God.

**Gabriel:** The third to deliver The 33 Lessons; an archangel.

**God:** The One, the Now, the Source, Presence, cosmic consciousness, the universe, the One in which we are all One.

**Guru:** A holy person, master, or spiritual teacher, especially in Indian and Eastern traditions.

**Hajam:** The spirit guide who delivered The Truths.

**"Hava Nagila":** A Hebrew folk song of celebration.

**Higher self:** The concept of a more evolved spirit self that exists in the subconscious.

**Highest good:** The concept of good for all.

**Holy Beings/Holy Ones:** All entities and beings who are sacred.

**Jesus:** In Christian theology, the son of God.

**Kirtan:** Call-and-response singing in the Eastern tradition.

**Koran:** The holy book of Islam. Also spelled Quran.

**Kundalini:** The spiritual energy path of the body, starting at the base of the spine and extending through seven chakras to the crown of the head.

**Life's path/life's purpose:** What we are each put on this earth to do to achieve soul growth.

**Lock into the hum:** The concept of energy vibration of the universe.

**Manifesting:** The act of bringing into awareness.

**Meditation:** A method of accessing the Divine through breath and stillness.

**Medium:** A person who receives messages from other realms.

**Metaphysics:** A branch of philosophy dealing with the cosmic realm.

**Miriam:** The second spirit guide to deliver The 33 Divine Lessons.

**Mind's eye:** The concept of a place in the body in which clairvoyant information is received.

**Multiple personality disorder:** A psychiatric disorder in which a person displays several distinct personalities.

**Mystic:** A person who practices the spiritual arts.

**Ouija:** Once-popular parlor game that uses a board with letters and numbers. The purpose was to receive messages from the spirit world.

**Planchette:** A tool used with a Ouija board.

**Prayer:** A method of petitioning, asking, or speaking to God from your heart; also a religious practice.

**Psychic:** A person with the innate skill of using intuition as a result of connection with the cosmic consciousness.

**Receiving:** The act of channeling information and guidance from spiritual entities and Holy Beings.

**Rumi:** Mystic poet of sixteenth-century Persia.

**Saints:** In Catholic and other Christian theology, humans who have become sacred through miracles or works.

**Self-levitate:** The ability to lift oneself off the ground through meditation.

**Shaman:** A mystic and/or healer who works in the natural and animal realm, especially in Native American traditions.

**Soft gaze:** A method used in trance and meditation for seeing what is directly in front of the viewer, without paying too much attention to it, and while at the same time having the ability to see what is in the room and beyond.

**Soul growth:** The purpose of our lives; the concept of spiritual growth as the goal of human life.

**Spirit guide:** An entity from the who communicates to and through us.

**Spiritualism:** A belief system popular in the late 1800s and early 1900s in America.

**Strands:** The clues, signs, and symbols that the Divine uses to move us along our life's path.

**Stream of consciousness:** A method of writing in which language arrives to the page without stopping for internal editing.

**String theory:** A concept of theoretical physics.

**Synchronicity:** A seemingly coincidental occurrence of events, as directed by universal flow.

**The Divine:** Another name for God.

**The Now:** The concept of the present time and God as being One and the same.

**The Source:** Another name for God.

**Torah:** The holy book of Judaism.

**Trance:** A mystic state defined by the ability to connect to and experience cosmic consciousness.

**Vocalized channeling:** A method of receiving in which messages are received from another entity through vocalized speech or sound.

**Walk blind:** The concept of moving forward without understanding what lies ahead.

**Window:** The concept of an open portal or place for communication between two or more realms.

# Bibliography

Burnham, Sophy. *A Book of Angels*. New York: Ballantine, 2004.

Byrne, Rhonda. *The Secret*. New York: Atria Books, 2006.

Cameron, Margaret. *The Seven Purposes: An Experience in Psychic Phenomena*. New York: Harper and Brothers Publishing, 1918.

Daniel, Terri. *A Swan in Heaven: Conversations Between Two Worlds*. Los Angeles, CA: First House Press, 2008.

Dass, Baba Ram. *Be Here Now*. Santa Fe, NM: Hanuman Foundation, 1971.

Fulghum, Robert. *All I Really Need to Know I Learned in Kindergarten*. New York: Ballantine, 2004.

Harvey, Andrew. *The Direct Path*. New York: Broadway, 2000.

Hicks, Esther, and Jerry Hicks. *The Law of Attraction*. Carlsbad, CA: Hay House, 2006.

Kafka, Franz. *The Metamorphosis*. Tr. Ian Johnston. West Valley City, UT: Walking Lion Press, 2006.

Katz, Debra Lynne. *You Are Psychic*. St. Paul, MN: Llewellyn Publications, 2004.

Kuhn, Thomas S. *The Structure of Scientific Revolutions*. Chicago: University of Chicago Press, 1962.

M.A. (Oxon) [William Stainton Moses]. *Spirit Teachings*. London: The Psychological Press Association, 1883.

Moody, Fred. *Seattle and the Demons of Ambition*. New York: St. Martin's Griffin, 2004.

Moss, Phillip Allen. *The Second Book of Proverbs*. lulu.com, 2007.

Roberts, Jane, and Robert F. Butts. *Seth Speaks: The Eternal Validity of the Soul*. San Rafael, CA: New World Library, 1994.

Schucman, Helen. *A Course in Miracles: Combined Volume*. Mill Valley, CA: Foundation for Inner Peace, 2007.

Virtue, Doreen. *Divine Guidance*. Los Angeles, CA: Renaissance Books, 1999.

Walsch, Neale Donald. *Conversations with God*. New York: Putnam, 1996.


FILMS

*Fantasia*. Walt Disney Studio, 1940.

Hay, Louise L. *You Can Heal Your Life*. Hay House, 2008.

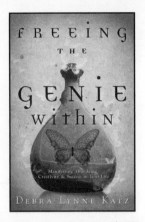

## FREEING THE GENIE WITHIN
### *Manifesting Abundance, Creativity & Success in Your Life*
#### DEBRA LYNNE KATZ

Get the perfect job, earn more money, and actualize all of your goals by developing your innate intuitive abilities. You have the power to attract anything you want right to your doorstep.

Refreshing and down-to-earth, *Freeing the Genie Within* is a unique and comprehensive training guide showing how to bust through emotional and metaphysical barriers and realize your full potential, using your psychic skills and the law of attraction.

These tailored techniques can be used every day, for every occasion. Try conscious breathing, positive affirmations, aura cleansing, meditation, and visualization exercises to supercharge your creativity, get off the treadmill of worry, knock out your fears, attract loving relationships, and build the life you've always wanted. Colored by Katz's personal anecdotes, this engaging book synthesizes methods of creativity, clairvoyance, and intention to make your dreams materialize.

978-0-7387-1475-2
336 pp., 5³⁄₁₆ x 8        $16.95

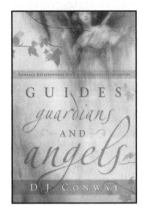

## GUIDES, GUARDIANS AND ANGELS
### *Enhance Relationships with Your Spiritual Companions*
### D. J. CONWAY

We may not see them. We may not hear them. But angels and spirit guides are with us all the time. Who are these entities? What is their purpose? How can we communicate with them?

*Guides, Guardians and Angels* is much more than an in-depth, cross-cultural exploration of these otherworldly beings. D. J. Conway reveals the role of these spiritual companions play and demonstrates how to develop a relationship with them through meditation, chants, rituals, and spells.

Take a fascinating tour of the multilayered Otherworld. Catch a glimpse of life between lives. Discover how power animals, nature spirits, dragons, light and shadow angels, and the spirits of friends, family, and pets fit into the spiritual equation. Revolutionize your understanding of Lucifer and other "fallen" angels. And learn from Conway's own personal experiences, which reinforce the profound impact these spirit teachers can have on our lives.

978-0-7387-1124-9
192 pp., 6 x 9          $17.95

# THE HAPPY MEDIUM
## *Awakening to Your Natural Intuition*
### JODI LIVON

What is it like to be a medium? Now is your chance to learn from a pro! With wit and candor, intuitive coach Jodi Livon shares the hard-won wisdom she's acquired on her fascinating journey as a psychic medium.

Over the years, Livon has helped clients, friends, family, and the dead find healing and learn life lessons. These true and incredibly touching stories not only illuminate spirit communication, but also offer guidance on tuning in to your own intuition. By relating how she receives and interprets psychic impressions, Livon shows firsthand how the psychic process works. With tips on trusting your senses, maintaining emotional balance, staying grounded, and interpreting signs from the universe, *The Happy Medium* can help you ignite your natural intuitive insights for higher awareness and guidance in life's decisions.

978-0-7387-1463-9
312 pp., 6 x 9          $16.95

## CRAFTING MAGICK WITH PEN AND INK
### *Learn to Write Stories, Spells, and Other Magickal Works*
### SUSAN PESZNECKER

Would you like to craft your own Book of Shadows? Create a ritual or spell for a special occasion? And ultimately infuse your writing with added beauty, style, and power? Just dip your quill into the deep wells of magick and creativity—and let the sparks of inspiration fly!

Empower your pen as you respond to the writing prompts and explore the techniques in this down-to-earth guide to magickal writing. Learn to write from the ground up with step-by-step instructions that take you through each stage of the creative process: brainstorming topics, freewriting, choosing a composition form, writing a rough draft, and revising your work to a refined polish. Sprinkled throughout are enjoyable exercises, helpful tips and terms, and inspiring writing samples to help you hone your craft. Whatever your medium—poetry, stories, spells, chants, prayers, blessings, or rituals—this book synthesizes the exciting realms of magick and writing to make your words truly come alive.

**978-0-7387-1145-4**
**264 pp., 6 x 9          $16.95**

## BRIDGE TO THE AFTERLIFE
### *A Medium's Message of Hope & Healing*
#### TROY PARKINSON

What if you could talk to the other side? What would you say? And what messages would the spirits have for you?

Spiritual medium Troy Parkinson, a rising star in the paranormal world, shares fascinating first-hand stories of his communications with the spirit realm.

Channeling spirits was the last thing that Troy Parkinson ever thought he'd do. A North Dakota native and self-described "ordinary guy," he first attended a spiritualist meeting when he was a college student in Boston. After receiving a message that night from his grandmother's spirit, he decided to pursue mediumship training through the world-renowned First Spiritual Temple of Boston. Parkinson now travels around the country, doing readings for large audiences and presenting workshops that teach people how to develop their own spirit-communication abilities. Troy's moving story and amazing messages from spirit will touch your heart, inspire your soul, and remind you that your loved ones are always with you.

978-0-7387-1435-6
240 pp., 6 x 9          $15.95

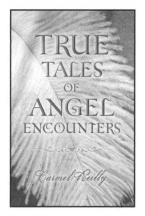

# True Tales of Angel Encounters
## Carmel Reilly

A distraught mother thinks twice about abandoning her family, a junkie is inspired to kick the habit, and a young man on the verge of insanity makes a remarkable recovery—thanks to the divine intervention of angels.

Ordinary people of diverse faiths, including the non-religious, have experienced the wonder of angels. This inspiring collection of true accounts highlights how these spiritual beings—manifesting as a kind stranger, a radiant figure, a gentle voice, or a comforting presence—have touched lives around the world. Breathtaking and heartwarming, these personal tales offer a convincing glimpse of angels at work—protecting children, offering advice during a crisis, healing babies, comforting the bereft and the dying, bringing messages from loved ones who have passed on, easing pain, and offering strength at the darkest hour.

*True Tales of Angel Encounters* is a glorious exploration of the human/angel relationship that's sure to reinvigorate your faith in the Divine.

978-0-7387-1494-3
312 pp., 5³⁄₁₆ x 8     $15.95

## LETTING GO
### *A Little Bit at a Time*
#### GUY FINLEY

With more than 200,000 copies sold, Guy Finley's international bestseller *The Secret of Letting Go* has touched people around the world. Now the best of Finley's message of hope and self-liberation is available in an attractive gift book format.

This portable treasury of wisdom from Llewellyn's best-selling self-help book presents an empowering quote for each day of the year. It features a new introduction by the author, inspirational photos, and comes in a handy take-anywhere size. *Letting Go: A Little Bit at a Time* makes it easy to let go of fear and reach a new kind of self-understanding that leads to true happiness.

**978-0-7387-1432-5**
**384 pp., 4¼ x 4¼**     **$9.95**

# BRINGING YOUR SOUL TO LIGHT
## *Healing Through Past Lives and the Time Between*
### DR. LINDA BACKMAN

What happens after we die? What is the purpose of my current life? Have I lived before?

In this unique and inspiring guide, Dr. Linda Backman answers these questions with compassion, objectivity, and more than thirty years of experience conducting traditional and past-life regression therapy with clients. *Bringing Your Soul to Light* includes a wealth of first-hand accounts from actual past-life and between-life regression sessions, offering readers a compelling and personal glimpse into the immortality of the soul.

Readers will discover the extraordinary universal connections we all share in this lifetime and beyond. They'll learn how they can use this knowledge to heal and grow, both physically and spiritually, by understanding themselves on a soul level and releasing energetic remnants of past-life trauma. *Bringing Your Soul to Light* includes a foreword by holistic healing pioneer and author C. Norman Shealy, M.D., Ph.D.

**978-0-7387-1321-2**
**264 pp., 6 x 9**          **$16.95**

# To Write to the Author

If you wish to contact the author or would like more information about this book, please write to the author in care of Llewellyn Worldwide and we will forward your request. Both the author and publisher appreciate hearing from you and learning of your enjoyment of this book and how it has helped you. Llewellyn Worldwide cannot guarantee that every letter written to the author can be answered, but all will be forwarded. Please write to:

Sara Wiseman
c/o Llewellyn Worldwide
2143 Wooddale Drive, Dept. 978-0-7387-1581-0
Woodbury, MN 55125-2989, U.S.A.

Please enclose a self-addressed stamped envelope for reply,
or $1.00 to cover costs. If outside U.S.A., enclose
international postal reply coupon.

Many of Llewellyn's authors have websites with additional information and resources. For more information, please visit our website at www.llewellyn.com